Presented to

By

On the Occasion of

Date

ISBN 1-58660-952-1

Published by Barbour Publishing, Inc., P.O. Box 719, Uhrichsville, Ohio 44683, www.barbourbooks.com

 Member of the
Evangelical Christian
Publishers Association

Printed in the United States of America.
5 4 3 2 1

JUST CALL ME MOM

Encouraging Words for Christian Mothers

BARBOUR
PUBLISHING

INTRODUCTION

Like you, I have had many titles in my life: Mom, mother-in-law, wife, friend, customer, patient, pain in the neck, and others along those lines. I'm sure there are plenty I will never know about if people are careful and, just maybe, a few of those are positive.

Titles do not make the woman. They are a shortcut for the speaker. It's easier to say "Laura's mom" than "daughter of Blanche and Ralph, wife of William, mother of Laura, Jim, and Steven," although the last system is certainly more precise and closer to the real meaning of the word *name*.

For the last thirty-seven years, my favorite title has been "Mom," followed closely by "Grandmother." I did other things over those thirty-seven years, including working outside the home to help pay for college, volunteer work, and working as a freelance editor, but nothing I found to do ever felt as right as being someone's mom.

Moms need all the help they can get. They rarely finish the daily work they have planned because of interruptions and emergencies. They are under constant stress, and the rewards they receive are elusive—(a child's quick hug)—and not lasting—(a clean kitchen floor). This book is meant to give you a quick break. You can read an entire devotion in a minute or two and then think about it while setting the table (or while trying to get your son to set it). The selections are from books by writers with years of experience as both Christians and mothers. We trust they will touch your heart, bring you closer to the Lord, and give you the peace you are seeking in your daily walk with God.

TONI SORTOR, Compiler

I DEDICATE MY HEART TO THE LORD

Search me, O God, and know my heart;
test me and know my anxious thoughts.
See if there is any offensive way in me,
and lead me in the way everlasting.

PSALM 139:23–24 NIV

*F*ather, I give You my heart, my soul, my life. I dedicate my whole being to You. I give You my failures and my successes, my fears and my aspirations.

Search my heart. Let my thoughts and motives be pure. You know me through and through. Remove the unclean ways in me that I might be pleasing to You.

Fill me with Your spirit, I pray; enable me to do the tasks set before me. Lead me into Your everlasting way.

Wherever I go, whatever the challenge, I pray that You will be there, guiding me completely. From my rising in the morn to my resting at night, O Lord, be near, surrounding me continually with Your love.

I look forward with joyful anticipation to what You have planned for me. Thank You for becoming Lord of my life.

We must remember God knows our future; He has our concerns and best interests at heart. Along the way we may not understand the reasoning of His direction for us. As we continue walking by faith in the paths He blazes, we'll learn His answers.

From *When I'm on My Knees*
BY ANITA CORRINE DONIHUE

MY MOTHER

The older women. . .can train the younger women
to love their husbands and children,
to be self-controlled and pure,
to be busy at home, to be kind.

TITUS 2:3–5 NIV

If my mother had been a different woman, I would be a different person. When she read to me each night, I learned about the world of words; today I make my living writing—and I still love coming home from the library with a stack of books to keep me company. When my mother took me outdoors and named the trees and flowers and birds for me, I learned about the world of nature. Today, whenever I'm upset or discouraged, I still find peace walking in the woods, and when I recognize ash and beech, trilliums and hepatica, purple finches and indigo buntings, I feel as though I'm saying the names of dear, old friends. And when my mother prayed with me each night and before each meal, I learned about an eternal world; today I seek God's presence daily and offer up my life to Him in prayer.

My mother trained me well.

From *Just the Girls*
BY ELLYN SANNA

THE DAYS OF YOUR YOUTH

Remember also your Creator in the days of your youth,
before the evil days come and the years draw near
when you will say, "I have no delight in them."
Fear God and keep His commandments,
because this applies to every person.
For God will bring every act to judgment,
everything which is hidden, whether it is good or evil.

ECCLESIASTES 12:1, 13–14 NASB

*M*ost of us have encountered women who freely share biblical truths "handed down to them" from their grandmothers or mothers. Is the faith being displayed in their lives?

The Book of Ecclesiastes concludes with the admonition not only to remember our Creator when we are young but to continue following His precepts throughout our time on earth. For nothing is sadder than to see those who began the race of life with so much vigor and potential now sitting on the sidelines watching the parade pass by.

High school reunions are great places to witness such scenes. Those girls whose faces glowed with extraordinary promise at eighteen may now display ones that appear more like a map of New York City. They've been betrayed, besieged, and bewildered by people promising much and delivering little.

Have you forgotten the God of your youth? Have His principles been compromised away by the pressures of a world that teaches the Ten Commandments are optional? With the Lord's help, it's not too late to turn it all around.

From *Daily Wisdom for Women*
BY CAROL L. FITZPATRICK

FINDING THE RIGHT COURSE

Therefore, if anyone is in Christ,
he is a new creation;
the old has gone,
the new has come!

2 Corinthians 5:17 niv

Perhaps you are at a turning point in your life, trying to decide which way to go. God has a wonderful adventure in store for you—if you are willing to give your all and place your life in His capable hands.

The same God who is able to move mountains, rivers, and even ocean waves is tenderly reaching out and inviting you to follow Him. Choose His course. Learn from Him. Obey Him. Draw close to Him and grow spiritually. Then experience His tender love and His tremendous power working in your life.

God has a new adventure awaiting me every day. He opens doors I never dreamed possible. He heals my hurts. He cares for my concerns. He frees me from fear. He transforms my temptations to triumph. Best of all, He gives me abundant life in all circumstances with a deep, endless joy from His Holy Spirit. For this, I never cease to thank Him.

From *When I Hear His Call*
by Anita Corrine Donihue

NO FEAR

If ye had known me,
ye should have known my Father also:
and from henceforth ye know him,
and have seen him.

JOHN 14:7 KJV

A friend of mine told me that her childhood was passed in a perfect terror of God. Her idea of Him was that He was a cruel giant with an awful "Eye" which could see everything, no matter how it might be hidden, and that He was always spying upon her and watching for chances to punish her, and to snatch away all her joys.

With a child's strange reticence she never told anyone of her terror; but one night Mother. . .heard the poor little despairing cry. . . and told her God was not a dreadful tyrant to be afraid of but was just like Jesus; and that she knew how good and kind Jesus was, and how He loved little children, and took them in His arms and blessed them. . . . When she heard that God was like Him, it was a perfect revelation to her and took away her fear of God forever. She went about all that day saying to herself over and over, "Oh, I am so glad I have found out that God is like Jesus, for Jesus is so nice. Now I need never be afraid of God anymore."

The little child had got a sight of God "in the face of Jesus Christ," and it brought rest to her soul.

HANNAH WHITALL SMITH
From *A Gentle Spirit*
COMPILED BY ASHLEIGH BRYCE CLAYTON

NOT A WORD

If the LORD be God, follow him:
but if Baal, then follow him.

1 KINGS 18:21 KJV

*T*he ball is in your court. Now is the time for you to respond, to let your testimony be known. What will you do? What will you say?

Elijah challenged the crowd (those 450 prophets of Baal, the 400 prophets of the groves, and all the kingdom of Israel) to make their choice.

What did they say? They answered him not a word. Not one individual in the crowd was willing to stand up and be counted for the Lord God.

What they did not consider was that God desired each individual to turn away from Baal and give allegiance to Him.

God challenges every heart to turn away from sin, to face Him, to follow Him. He desires to see my face, to hear my voice. I need to look Him right in the eye and affirm: Lord, You are God alone. You are God of all creation and God of my life. By Your grace I choose to follow You.

I need never be ashamed to make my allegiance to God public. I ought never be too frightened of humans to take a stand for eternal God, never too preoccupied to find time to honor and worship Him. Never do I want to have to confess that I had an opportunity to give reason for my faith but answered not a word.

From *All I Have Needed*
BY ELVA MINETTE MARTIN

A LOVING TOUCH

"Now that I, your Lord and Teacher,
have washed your feet,
you also should wash one another's feet.
I have set you an example that
you should do as I have done for you.
I tell you the truth,
no servant is greater than his master,
nor is a messenger greater than
the one who sent him.
Now that you know these things,
you will be blessed if you do them."

JOHN 13:14–17 NIV

*I*t was the end of a long night's work on my job in a fast-food restaurant. Standing on concrete night after night had taken its toll. I was getting bone spurs in the bottom of each foot.

Our oldest son, Bob Jr., was visiting from out of town. When I arrived home, he was waiting up for me. I stepped through the living room door, sank to the couch, and kicked off my work shoes.

As Bob and I began visiting, he sat down beside me and took my feet in his hands. Ever so gently, he began massaging them. I recoiled at the mere thought of his touching my sweaty feet. He never paused but kept rubbing and listening to me tell about my night's work. I think that was one of the greatest acts of love I have ever experienced, one I will treasure and never forget.

From *When God Calls Me Blessed*
BY ANITA CORRINE DONIHUE

OUR GROWN CHILDREN AND THEIR MATES

Be kind and compassionate to one another,
forgiving each other,
just as in Christ God forgave you.

EPHESIANS 4:32 NIV

I watch in awe as my grown children go about their duties. When did they become so wise, Lord? I must have done some things right. My sons and daughters-in-law are a blessing. Thank You for the love they have for each other and for us, their parents.

I hear our sons and daughters-in-law share some of the same things with their children I once taught them. I see them looking for the best in the children, continually lifting them up and praising their efforts, even as I did and do. How wonderful.

Although our sons are grown, Lord, they are still our kids. So are their wives and children. Thank You for reminding me to still look for the good in all of them and to encourage them. Each day, I pray for You to give them help and strength. I ask Your loving protection to surround them, molding them to Your will.

Thank You for nudges to do and say things or to stay quiet. I gratefully lean on Your wisdom while You show me how to be a blessing as a parent of our grown kids who still need lots of love.

From *When I'm Praising God*
BY ANITA CORRINE DONIHUE

NAMES

A GOOD name is rather to be chosen than great riches.

PROVERBS 22:1 KJV

*O*h, no, it's raining! . . ." My three-year-old hand flew to my forehead.

"Yes, Miss Drama." My mother smiled and shook her head. "I should have named you Greta, after a famous actress." Somehow, the name stuck. . . .

When I was a small child, my mother was simply "Mommy." As I grew older, though, her name changed to "Mom." Then one night at dinner I nicknamed her.

"Gracias, Madre," I said as she filled my bowl with her homemade chili. . . . From then on, we used our nicknames for each other.

And then one day, out of the blue, my mother changed her name again. I still remember the phone call.

"Donna," she began, "I've regressed twenty-five years. From now on you might as well call me Helen."

"What did you do?"

"I had my ears pierced."

My next visit home I handed her a gift. "Helen, this is to honor your new youthful image," I told her. Every time she wore those earrings, I swelled with pride and joy. And I can imagine the following scene when I go to heaven:

"God, where is my mother? You know—Helen. She's probably wearing white feather earrings."

"Oh, you mean Madre?"

"Yes!"

"She's right here waiting for you, Greta."

DONNA LANGE
From *Just the Girls*
BY ELLYN SANNA

THE RAINBOW

"I have set my rainbow in the clouds,
and it will be the sign of the covenant
between me and the earth."

GENESIS 9:13 NIV

*B*efore sunrise the rain beat furiously against our trailer, rousing me from a deep sleep. Once it subsided the birds chirped sweetly and I raised the window shade to peek outside. Stretching boldly across the gray clouds lay a vibrant semicircle of color. And slightly above it arched another, more muted bow. "God, You really outdid Yourself this time!" I shouted, waking my husband who reluctantly nodded and then threw the covers over his head. A minute later I flew out the door for a better vantage point.

Every day God freely displays His blessings. Are we too busy or disinterested to appreciate their wonder? Even if we've forgotten He's there, reminders are all around, for He is the God of covenants. In a world where promises (or covenants) are disregarded routinely, I need God's kind of stability.

Have you ever made a covenant or a vow to God only to find that life's circumstances prevented you from keeping it? Perhaps it was a marriage vow. In my own marriage there have been times when just honoring that vow has taken every bit of courage and strength I have. Without God's intervention my stubborn flesh would never stay one more day and watch for His miracles of change and hope.

From *Daily Wisdom for Women*
BY CAROL L. FITZPATRICK

OUR ADVOCATE AND DEFENDER

"Therefore everyone who confesses Me before men,
I will also confess him before My Father who is in heaven."

MATTHEW 10:32 NASB

My sisters and I attended private schools for most of our lives but that did not render us immune to rowdies or bullies. And since we walked a few miles to school each day, we were at times easy prey.

Busy with friends her own age, my older sister didn't usually accompany my younger sister and me on our morning trek.

However, when we returned home one day relating that two big kids from the nearby public school had threatened to beat us up the next day, she rallied to the cause. As she instructed, we traversed our normal route while she lagged watchfully a short distance behind.

Suddenly the two boys jumped out of the bushes ahead. And just like a superwoman, our sister pounced on them, easily overpowering both and giving them bloody noses in the process. I'll never forget that scene as long as I live. It felt so incredible to have an invincible defender!

If we know Jesus Christ and have responded to His invitation to receive Him as Savior, Jesus remains forever our advocate before the Father, saying with love, "She's mine." Know that you are so precious to Jesus that He gave His life for you. Doesn't it feel incredible to have Jesus as your defender?

From *Daily Wisdom for Women*
BY CAROL L. FITZPATRICK

WHERE DO YOU TAKE REFUGE?

When I am afraid, I will put my trust in You.
In God, whose word I praise,
In God I have put my trust;
I shall not be afraid.
What can mere man do to me?

PSALM 56:3–4 NASB

When my father was away during World War II, my mom, sister, and I lived with my grandparents. At the time I was only three years old or so. Frequently, I'd hide under their long, wooden porch, making my world a little smaller, I suppose. Looking out through the latticed covering, somehow I felt safe.

David wrote this psalm when the Philistines had seized him in Gath. These Philistines had been enemies of the Israelites for a long time. At one point they'd even stolen the Ark of the Covenant. They'd probably never forgiven David for killing their giant, Goliath. I wonder if David reflected during his present predicament, remembering the time in his youth when he'd faced that giant with only five smooth stones and a sling. He had called upon his God to deliver him, and the Lord had prevailed (1 Samuel 17:37–50).

Where do you go for refuge? I run to the arms of my loving Father, just as David did in his own crisis. And He always comes through.

From *Daily Wisdom for Women*
BY CAROL L. FITZPATRICK

AN ABUNDANT CHILDHOOD

*"A man's life does not consist in
the abundance of his possessions."*

LUKE 12:15 NIV

$\mathscr{W}$e were pretty poor when I was a child, but I didn't know that until I was a teenager and someone told me. I knew both my parents worked, and our cars were always secondhand, and if I wanted spending money I had to work for it, but I was never hungry, and our apartment was always clean.

All the kids in our neighborhood played together, running from yard to yard in contests of make-believe or playing baseball in the empty lot. We played outside in all weather until our faces went numb or we needed a snack of cereal or apples to keep us going. We took care of one another the best we could until dinnertime or darkness.

Life was simple. The strongest ruled with compassion, although the smartest made most of the rules. The weakest were allowed their turn, and nobody knew or cared what their parents made. If you had fifteen cents for a cola and glazed donut, you were rich enough. If you didn't, someone would share with you. If we were reasonably cautious, we were always safe, and any danger we met was of our own making, not from the world around us. We lived truly abundant lives as children.

From *Everyday Abundance*
BY TONI SORTOR

I HAVE OTHER THINGS TO DO

Redeeming the time, because the days are evil.

EPHESIANS 5:16 KJV

I have other things to do. . .too much to get finished before bedtime.

But here I am, with a baby on my lap, going round and round and up and down on a carousel. Behind me, my six year old lectures his younger brother and sister about merry-go-rounds and carousels, about horse tails and whatever else captures his fleeting fancy. . . . The kids get off the ride with new energy, eager to explore.

"Let's go to the castle! . . ." They have been to this park countless times, but to them it is new again. After all, it is a new day.

I watch them wistfully. Oh, to have the eyes of a child to see the world fresh each day! To have a child's mind that neither lingers on the past nor frets about the future. . . .

To children, life is "now." And they are right. Life is now. We are promised nothing beyond this moment. Marriage and motherhood—and childhood—are not forever, but for now. Yet if we miss them now, we will have missed them forever.

They run to the playground near the mill.

"Mommy! Watch me!"

"Mommy! Push me!"

I lift my preschooler into the swing and give a push.

"I'm fwinging!" she laughs. "Higher!"

I give another push. And another.

Yes, I have other things to do.

But none better.

From *Lessons for a SuperMom*
BY HELEN WIDGER MIDDLEBROOKE

MOTHERLY THREATS

Visiting the iniquity of the fathers upon the children,
and upon the children's children,
unto the third and to the fourth generation.

EXODUS 34:7 KJV

The experts say it is unwise to threaten children. But every mother does it.

My mother had the usual arsenal of threats: "Do that, and you'll put your eye out."

"Someday your face will freeze like that."

We knew she never meant them. And we knew they never came true—except for one.

I don't remember what I was doing that day, but it must have been bad. . . . When her eyes narrowed. . .I should have known it was too late.

She looked at me with fiery eyes and let me have it: "May you have a child just like you."

So far, I have six who are "just like me."

This curse can't fail because when we reproduce, we reproduce more than bodies. We reproduce our attitudes and values in our children. For better or worse, they will be like we are.

One day, the stubborn, asthmatic, short-tempered one was nagging me with his latest idea to spend my money. . . .

My eyes narrowed, and my jaw tightened: "May you have a child just like you!"

He stiffened and paled.

I know, it was cruel.

But he had it coming.

From *Lessons for a SuperMom*
BY HELEN WIDGER MIDDLEBROOKE

MY FAMILY

Finally, all of you,
live in harmony with one another;
be sympathetic, love as brothers,
be compassionate and humble.

1 PETER 3:8 NIV

*F*ather, thank You for my family and for the love that flows between us. We are all so different, yet each constantly bridges the gaps and relates to one another.

The precious gift of my family comes from You. Thank You for reminding me never to take them for granted and for nourishing my family's love so we remain close.

When things become strained among any of us, I praise You that I can take each loved one to You and ask for help and wisdom. I never cease to be amazed at the way You give insight so I can see things from my other family members' points of view.

Thank You for the holidays, birthdays, barbecues, and picnics. Thank You, too, for the quiet one-on-one walks and talks. Some of these I will cherish for years to come.

My family isn't perfect, but I don't love them for perfection. I love them in spite of their faults. I love them because they are my family, planned for me before we ever came into being. Thank You, Father, for each one.

From *When I'm Praising God*
BY ANITA CORRINE DONIHUE

DIFFICULTIES CONCERNING FAITH

Jesus said unto him,
If thou canst believe,
all things are possible to him that believeth.

MARK 9:23 KJV

I wish you would try to imagine yourself acting in your human relations as you do in your spiritual relations. Suppose you should begin tomorrow with the notion in your head that you could not trust anybody because you had no faith. When you sat down to breakfast you would say, "I cannot eat anything on this table, for I have no faith, and I cannot believe the cook has not put poison in the coffee, or that the butcher has not sent home diseased or unhealthy meat"; so you would go away starving. When you went out to your daily avocations, you would say, "I cannot ride in the railway train, for I have no faith. . . ."

Just picture such a day as this, and see how disastrous it would be to yourself, and what utter folly it would appear to anyone who should watch you through the whole of it. . . And then ask yourself the question, "If this want of faith in your fellowmen would be so dreadful, and such utter folly, what must it be when you tell God that you have no power to trust Him, nor to believe His word; that it is a great trial, but you cannot help it, 'for you have no faith'?"

HANNAH WHITALL SMITH
From *A Gentle Spirit*
COMPILED BY ASHLEIGH BRYCE CLAYTON

IN THE LORD JESUS, I BELIEVE

I know whom I have believed,
and am persuaded that he is able to keep that which
I have committed unto him against that day.

2 TIMOTHY 1:12 KJV

I believe in You, Lord Jesus. Thank You for helping me not to be tossed to and fro on the gusts of fads, new gimmicks, or propaganda. If not for You, I would be like a wandering sheep.

Thank You for helping me to seek and know Your truth. I praise You for giving me intelligence to search out right from wrong. Your Word is a lamp to my feet and a light to my path. I praise You for leading. Through You, my life has become richer and fuller with a deep, inner joy.

No matter what happens, no matter the influences, in You I will still believe and live.

Thank You for walking ahead of me, so I may follow; for walking beside me, so I may know Your fellowship; for staying close behind me, so I may be protected. Each time I hear Your voice, I will follow.

In You, I believe. In You, I trust. In You, Lord Jesus, are all of life's answers. You, my true God, are sufficient! I need no other.

From *When I'm Praising God*
BY ANITA CORRINE DONIHUE

GETTING TO KNOW
THE LORD BETTER

"As surely as the sun rises, he will appear;
he will come to us like the winter rains,
like the spring rains that water the earth."

HOSEA 6:3 NIV

I delight in Your presence, O Lord. As I commune with You, I am getting to know You better. Yet I still know only a tiny morsel of Your magnificent ways. . . .

When I come to You, I'm blessed by Your glorious presence, like the dawning of a new day. Your spirit refreshes and overflows on me like a soft spring rain. I tilt my head up to You and feel washed—cleaner than freshly fallen snow. Time and time again, You have shown me Your faithfulness. I am learning to let the worries go and thank You for the answers. When I obey, You fill me with joy and peace far greater than I can ever describe. . . .

My life is like a symphony as long as I am tuned to Your will. I bring my rebellious nature repeatedly and place it at Your feet. Please help me be pliable while You remold my stubborn will into something steadfast, lovely, and good, to be used by You.

What delight I have in all You do in my life, Lord! I can hardly wait to see what You have in store for me next. I trust You. My past, my present, and my future I commit to You. You are my life, my all.

From *When I'm Praising God*
BY ANITA CORRINE DONIHUE

SELF-DENIAL

And he saith unto them,
Follow me,
and I will make you fishers of men.

MATTHEW 4:19 KJV

*S*elf-denial has to do primarily with my will. It is a willingness to say yes to the lordship of Jesus in my life, to do what He asks of me to the best of my ability, even if I have made other plans. God will not request more of me than I can handle. He knows my limits. I need to submit my life to God's leading, to be willing to step out in faith. That's not easy. Paul says I am to present myself a living sacrifice to God (Romans 12:1). But as someone else said, the problem with living sacrifices is that they keep crawling off the altar!

The only thing that works for me is to take my eyes off myself and put them on Jesus. If I am always looking inward, either to defend myself or to see if I'm really denying myself, I get nowhere. Then "I'm so busy with me that I have no time for you."

Remember that Jesus gave us three steps, not just one: Deny myself, take up my cross, and follow Him. It's that third condition of discipleship that motivates me. When Jesus called His twelve disciples, He called them to follow Him. He didn't organize a committee meeting and draw up a contract for them to sign that outlined the job description and benefits package. He simply said, "Follow Me." What this involves is keeping my eyes on Him, walking where He leads, and obeying Him moment by moment.

From *Created for a Purpose*
BY DARLENE SALA

26

TO TOUCH JESUS' CLOAK

*A woman who had had a hemorrhage for twelve years,
and had endured much at the hands of many physicians,
and had spent all that she had and was not helped at all,
but rather had grown worse—after hearing about Jesus
she came up in the crowd behind Him, and touched His
cloak. For she thought, "If I just touch His garments,
I will get well."*

MARK 5:25–28 NASB

This woman is frantic. Each time she's received the report of a gifted healer, she's traversed far and wide to find a cure. The wonder is that this dear woman could survive for twelve long years. For that phrase, "endured much," means she "suffered something or experienced evil."

In one last-ditch effort she reaches out to touch the garment of Jesus as He passes by. She doesn't bother to call out to Him or even ask for help. Somehow she knows that His very holiness can heal her physically.

"Immediately Jesus, perceiving in Himself that the power proceeding from Him had gone forth, turned around in the crowd and said, 'Who touched My garments?'" (Mark 5:30 NASB). The disciples think He's "losing it" for sure.

"But the woman fearing and trembling, aware of what had happened to her, came and fell down before Him and told Him the whole truth" (Mark 5:33 NASB). She's been miraculously healed, and now she demonstrates her faith by worshiping at Jesus' feet. Does your faith shine through even in small gestures?

From *Daily Wisdom for Women*
BY CAROL L. FITZPATRICK

NEVERTHELESS I WILL

That we may lead a quiet and peaceable life
in all godliness and honesty.
For this is good and acceptable in
the sight of God our Saviour;
Who will have all men to be saved, and to come unto the
knowledge of the truth.

1 TIMOTHY 2:2–4 KJV

*I*f we truly love, revere, and trust God, we will continue to honor Him in bad or hard times, just as we do in the midst of good and pleasant times. Evidently Obadiah did so. Jezebel executed the prophets of God, probably to try to do away with Elijah, but Obadiah hid one hundred prophets of God in caves and faithfully provided bread and water for their sustenance.

Elijah promised Obadiah in God's name that he would surely present himself to Ahab that very day. So Obadiah carried the announcement back to his employer.

In the Gospel of Luke, it is related that Jesus told Peter to cast his net on the right side of the ship, and he would catch fish. Peter had reason not to obey, for he had been casting his net into the water repeatedly all night long and pulling it back in empty! But he concluded: "Nevertheless at thy word I will let down the net" (Luke 5:5 KJV).

So did Obadiah. Though he first complained and hesitated in fear, he yielded to God's will, returning to meet the king and delivering Elijah's message.

From *All I Have Needed*
BY ELVA MINETTE MARTIN

PERSEVERANCE

*May the Lord direct your hearts into
God's love and Christ's perseverance.*

2 THESSALONIANS 3:5 NIV

Suffering, says Paul, teaches us perseverance. That means we learn to "stick with it." We don't give up easily; we just keep on plugging on. Just as water will eventually wear away stone, the ability to keep going in the end will accomplish great things.

William Carey, a nineteenth-century missionary to India, knew just how important perseverance is to God's kingdom. Year after year, in the face of failure after failure, Carey kept going—and eventually, he brought great changes to India as he spread the gospel there. He explained his life this way: "I can plod. That is my only genius. I can persevere in any definite pursuit. To this I owe everything."

Most of us think that great talents and perfect achievement would be more use to God. But through perseverance we learn hope, a hope that is firmly based in Jesus Christ. William Carey's motto was this: "Attempt great things for God, expect great things from God." He knew that his own efforts would always disappoint him—but his hope in God would never be disappointed.

From *Created for a Purpose*
BY DARLENE SALA

OUR THOUGHTS

Whatsoever things are true,
whatsoever things are honest, whatsoever things are just,
whatsoever things are pure, whatsoever things are lovely,
whatsoever things are of good report;
if there be any virtue, and if there be any praise,
think on these things.

PHILIPPIANS 4:8 KJV

The things we think on are the things that feed our souls. If we think on pure and lovely things we shall grow pure and lovely like them; and the converse is equally true. Very few people at all realize this, and consequently there is a great deal of carelessness, even with careful people, in regard to their thoughts. They guard their words and actions with the utmost care, but their thoughts, which, after all, are the very spring and root of everything in character and life, they neglect entirely. So long as it is not put into spoken words, it seems of no consequence at all what goes on within the mind. No one hears or knows, and therefore they imagine that the vagrant thoughts that come and go as they list do no harm. Such persons are very careless as to the food offered to their thoughts and accept haphazardly, without discrimination, anything that comes.

Every thought we think. . .must be the thought Christ would think were He placed in our circumstances and subject to our conditions. This is what it really means to feed on Him.

HANNAH WHITALL SMITH
From *A Gentle Spirit*
COMPILED BY ASHLEIGH BRYCE CLAYTON

CONFIDENCE

*"For God so loved the world that
he gave his one and only Son,
that whoever believes in him
shall not perish but have eternal life."*

JOHN 3:16–17 NIV

*I*t's so easy to get ground down by circumstances to the point where we are unsure of everything and everyone. Whom can we trust today? Huge corporations fail, taking our retirement savings with them and leaving the security of our old age in doubt. Diseases once believed conquered reappear stronger than ever. Nothing is sure these days. At least that's how it feels.

Yet the Lord tells us, " 'And surely I am with you always, to the very end of the age' " (Matthew 28:20 NIV). " 'Do not be afraid. I am the First and the Last. I am the Living One; I was dead, and behold I am alive for ever and ever! And I hold the keys of death and Hades' " (Revelation 1:17–18 NIV).

Much of the time we must live with things the way they are because it is not in our power to change them, but when our confidence fails there is still someone we can cling to—the Lord who came to save us and loves us still. We may cling to Him in confidence, for He will never fail us. He is always there to lift us up again, to give us confidence and show us the path of love that leads us toward a hopeful future.

From *Everyday Abundance*
BY TONI SORTOR

THE OPEN DOOR

Where there is no vision, the people perish:
but he that keepeth the law, happy is he.

PROVERBS 29:18 KJV

*T*here is something about hesitation and reconsiderations that is curiously fatal to successful achievement. Good fortune is in going on—not in going back. The parable of Lot's wife, who turned into a pillar of salt because she looked back, is by no means inapplicable to the life of today. Let one on whom the vision has shone look backward instead of forward, and he becomes paralyzed and immovable. . . . He has withdrawn himself from all the heavenly forces that lead him on. The fidelity to the vision is the vital motor. It gives that exhilaration of energy which makes possible the impossible.

Each recurring New Year is an open door. However arbitrary are the divisions of time, there is inspiration and exaltation in standing on the threshold of an untried year, with its fresh pages awaiting record. It is, again, the era of possibilities. The imaginative faculty of the soul must, indeed, be "fed with objects immense and eternal." Life stretches before one in its diviner unity—even in the wholeness of the life that is and that which is to come. There is not one set of motives and purposes to be applied to this life, and another set to that which awaits us. This is the spiritual world, here and now. It is well to drop the old that one may seize the new.

LILIAN WHITING
From *A Gentle Spirit*
COMPILED BY ASHLEIGH BRYCE CLAYTON

THE CHRISTIAN FAMILY

Rejoice with them that do rejoice,
and weep with them that weep.
Be of the same mind one toward another.

ROMANS 12:15–16 KJV

*M*any of us love and appreciate our genealogical families. The bloodline ties are strong. The memories built are loved and cherished.

There is another kind of family. It's broader than the Jones or Smith family. It is the Christian family, one made by God, our Father. Here, too, is a strong bond of love.

We often refer to one another as brothers and sisters in Christ. Some members of the Christian family help parent the younger. Others form friendships that last a lifetime.

What causes this spiritual family bond with ties lasting into eternity? The bond comes from God adopting each of us as His own children. He pours out a love that spreads from one of us to the other. He often blesses people with His presence by working through the believers in His Christian family.

Love in God's family can even go as deep as our genealogical one. Frequently, praise God, the two interweave.

The family is God's holy Church. It may be shaken, split by division, or injured by illness or death. With God's healing presence, His family is restored and goes on.

The greatest miracle is we are not forever separated. We can look forward to being reunited with Christ in heaven.

From *When I'm in His Presence*
BY ANITA CORRINE DONIHUE

GRUMBLING

And do not grumble, as some of them did—
and were killed by the destroying angel.

1 CORINTHIANS 10:10 NIV

*E*vidently God sees grumbling as a lot more serious sin than I do. Did you know that He put it in the same category as idolatry and sexual immorality (1 Corinthians 10)? That certainly gets my attention!

The children of Israel were on their way from Egypt to the land God had promised them. Along the way things did not go like they expected—and they didn't hesitate to make sure Moses, their leader, knew exactly how they felt about things! They clearly had an "attitude," and. . .most of them died in the wilderness because they did not believe and obey God. Paul says, "Now these things occurred as examples, to keep us from setting our hearts on evil things as they did."

I'm glad the next verse is one of reassurance. God will help me the next time I'm tempted to complain, for He says: "God is faithful; he will not let you be tempted beyond what you can bear. But when you are tempted, he will also provide a way out so that you can stand up under it" (1 Corinthians 10:13 NIV).

From *Encouraging Words for Women*
BY DARLENE SALA

KEEP THE HOME FIRES BURNING

Blessed are all who fear the LORD, who walk in his ways.
You will eat the fruit of your labor;
blessings and prosperity will be yours.

PSALM 128:1–2 NIV

*F*ather, I have been rushing all week. It seems like everything I'm doing is for a worthy cause. Because I'm getting into overload and not having enough time with the ones I love the most, I canceled a meeting I was to attend tonight. Instead, my husband, family, and I are going to have an evening together. . . .

I want to serve You by helping others, but I know the ones who are to come first in my life. The meeting, along with many more, can manage without me.

Thank You for my family. How dear they are to me. I look at my loving husband and my "olive shoots," big and small, and praise You for these priceless blessings. Help me never to take them for granted. Time passes too quickly.

Remind me of my priorities, Father. Help me remember my foremost mission is at home. Teach me first to keep the home fires burning. Guide and help me each day to be a beacon of light to the ones I love the most. . . .

Place a spiritual hedge of thorns around them, Lord. Protect them from evil and harm. Let everything I say and do be a beacon of light to them, reflecting Your purity and love.

From *When God Calls Me Blessed*
BY ANITA CORRINE DONIHUE

LOVE COMES FROM THE LORD

A new commandment I give unto you,
That ye love one another;
as I have loved you, that ye also love one another.

JOHN 13:34 KJV

*L*ord, You often remind us to love and care for our families first. At times we American families are so busy being thoughtful to those outside our homes that we forget the ones who are most important. Our families deserve our best manners, our best attention, and our first love, second to God.

Instead, at times we forget our thoughtful and kind ways and mistreat each other. Perhaps we think our families will put up with our actions, because they love us "just the way we are." Must we play mind games or belittle and manipulate the ones we love? Must we say hurtful things to get our way or to get our points across? How sad. This must grieve You terribly, Lord. It is so wrong and so destructive. Forgive us for such sinful actions.

Help us treat our spouses, children, and other loved ones with kindness, to cherish and care for them. Help us to avoid careless words that may injure for a lifetime. May we treasure these dear ones and share their joys and concerns and dreams. May our foremost time and effort be with the ones we love the most. Let us show them the love we talk about so freely, so our families will grow strong and secure in You.

Lord, we know we cannot have strong family units without following Your teachings. You know our hearts. Let our lives please You.

From *When I'm on My Knees*
BY ANITA CORRINE DONIHUE

HELP ME FORGIVE

"Forgive, and you will be forgiven."

LUKE 6:37 NIV

I've been hurt again, Lord. Not only me, but the ones I love. I'm angry at the cruelty. I know there is no remorse. If the ones who hurt me had it to do again, they'd do the same things. I want to lash out. I want to get even. I know this isn't how You want me to react. My hatred and anger can harm many people, myself, and my relationship with You and others, Lord. I can't seem to forgive or change my attitudes. Please help me. I pray that You will take away my pain and wrong attitudes.

I've done all I can to work things out with no success. Now I seek Your direction and will. I know You command me to love and pray for others, even my enemies. Although their actions are wrong, help me to respond in the right way. Remind me not to rejoice when they meet trouble but to pray continually for them. Guard my tongue against speaking unkind words. Help me to have a pure heart and leave the rest in Your hands.

Because I submit to You, I sense Your help and peace in this situation. I'm learning how much love You must have to forgive me.

From *When I'm on My Knees*
BY ANITA CORRINE DONIHUE

IN THE GARDEN

When the woman saw that the tree was good for food,
and that it was a delight to the eyes,
and that the tree was desirable to make one wise,
she took from its fruit and ate;
and she gave also to her husband with her, and he ate.

GENESIS 3:6 NASB

On a day she'd never forget, Eve stood beside the "tree of the knowledge of good and evil" and began listening to the seductive voice of the crafty serpent. How could she know that this voice desired to entice her and Adam away from God and the security of the Garden of Eden? She innocently chose to ignore the truth of God's Word and obey that new voice.

And Adam, who loved her, listened to her voice. He then accepted her invitation to join her in partaking of the fruit of the tree. As a result, cloaked with garment skins of animals sacrificed to cover their sin, Adam and Eve were forced out of this physical garden paradise. Yet the echo of God's loving promise lingered in their ears. . .a Redeemer would come.

Two thousand years later, Jesus returned to another garden, choosing it as His place of prayer. Kneeling there, He would accomplish for men and women this task of abiding in the Father and obeying His commands. And on the cross the sacrifice of His life provided forgiveness, once again allowing access to God's presence. . .now within a spiritual garden of prayer.

From *Daily Wisdom for Women*
BY CAROL L. FITZPATRICK

TRAVELING LIGHT

*"Wear my yoke—for it fits perfectly—
and let me teach you;
for I am gentle and humble,
and you shall find rest for your souls;
for I give you only light burdens."*

MATTHEW 11:29–30 TLB

*I*t's tough for a woman to travel light. I shed unnecessary baggage about as fast as I discard cellulite. I can't help myself; preparedness is my motto.

In much the same way, we ladies often have trouble traveling light spiritually. Like hungry squirrels storing acorns for the winter, we store resentment to feed unforgiveness just in case we should need to defend ourselves, keep our distance, or establish our rights.

Some of us have hauled the backpack of anxiety and fear so long that worry has become second nature. Consequently, we fret about problems that are out of our control or circumstances we're unable to change.

Jesus, however, instructs us to shed the excess baggage of sin and negative emotions that weigh us down and encumber our journey. He provides rest from the heavy load long before we arrive at our final destination. The excess attitudes we tow through life are useless and destructive. That's why God instructs us to "throw off everything that hinders and the sin that so easily entangles" (Hebrews 12:1 NIV) before we allow our burdens to ruin life's trip.

From *Laughter Therapy*
BY TINA KRAUSE

NORTHERN DAWN

*"Your eyes will see the king in his beauty
and view a land that stretches afar."*

ISAIAH 33:17 NIV

I woke up fuzzy and disoriented until I heard the muffled thunk of the cruise ship's engines. It was light enough that I could clearly see my watch's face: 3:00 A.M.! Dawn was breaking, and I was wide awake, a victim of jet lag after a fourteen-hour flight to Alaska. I threw on a warm jacket and jeans and left my husband, who never gets jet lag, sleeping peacefully. Two short lefts and I was on the bow of the promenade deck, huddled up against a wall.

When a brand-new shaft of warm sunlight hit my face, I looked up and gasped. Spread before me was an Alaskan fjord. We floated on strange blue-green, semiopaque water; glaciers sparkled on the sides of the mountains that climbed straight out of the sea and up to the bottom of the clouds. Two quick rights and I was back in our cabin, shaking my husband. "Get up! You've got to see this!" A short while later there were about fifteen of us shivering and yawning on deck, whispering among ourselves, not wanting to wake up anyone else. This was our dawn—our beauty—we didn't need more company. A window opened above us, and a face looked down from the bridge. "Good morning, East Coasters. Coffee and Danish are in the lounge if you need them. Isn't it worth the fourteen-hour plane ride?"

Oh yes, it certainly was!

From *Everyday Abundance*
BY TONI SORTOR

MOOSE

God made the wild animals
according to their kinds, the livestock. . .
and all the creatures that move
along the ground according to their kinds.
And God saw that it was good.

GENESIS 1:25 NIV

I know that God has a sense of humor. He did, after all, create the moose, which looks like a horse gone incredibly wrong. I met my first moose in the middle of an isolated logging road. We made the mistake of rounding a blind bend a little too fast, coming face-to-knee with a young animal who stood his ground in true moose fashion. My first thought was, *He's so big!* Television or photographs do not convey the sheer massiveness of a moose—even a young one.

Moose are not overly intelligent. Fortunately, they are exceedingly calm, collected animals, curious and patient with humans who invade their space. This particular moose blocked the road for a good ten minutes to look us over before ambling off into the bushes on moose business.

No human who has ever shared space with a moose can avoid loving them. Their ugliness, their bony long legs, their cowlike eyes—you just can't resist them. They are somewhat like an ugly baby—always a surprise, but one that makes you smile in spite of yourself and thank God for providing such unexpected delight. God didn't make the moose beautiful or smart, just irresistible, and seeing a moose can only be considered a blessing.

From *Everyday Abundance*
BY TONI SORTOR

BEAR

The blessing of the LORD brings wealth,
and he adds no trouble to it.

PROVERBS 10:22 NIV

*I*t took years of vacationing in the woods before I saw my first bear in the wild. I'd seen the south end of a northbound bear as he dove into the bushes, but that didn't count. I'd seen bear tracks and bear scat and once caught the smell of a bear—unpleasant, to say the least—but never got a real look at one until an abnormal black smudge under a tree caught my attention. My guide slowed the truck to a crawl, and there the bear was, taking a nap in the shade on a hot summer day.

"Three hundred. . .three-fifty pounds," the guide estimated. The bear lifted his head and searched for our scent, didn't like what he smelled, and stood up. "He'll run," the guide predicted.

I was torn by two opposing desires. I could reach for my camera or keep my eyes on the bear and forget the picture. I voted for watching. So big, so powerful—there would be no getting out of the truck for a better view of this animal! The bear, still groggy from the sun, slowly turned and walked off into the woods, dismissing us as nothing to be concerned about. In less than a minute he'd been there and then was gone.

"You didn't get a picture?" the guide asked.

I pointed to my head. "I got him here. That's enough."

From *Everyday Abundance*
BY TONI SORTOR

FOG

"I am the light of the world.
Whoever follows me will never walk in darkness,
but will have the light of life."

JOHN 8:12 NIV

The float plane coming in to take us to another lake for a day's fishing was late, the reason obvious. Standing on the shore, we could not see the end of the dock through the fog. The pilot would be lucky just to find the lake. Soon we could hear him circling above us, searching for the one small, clear spot he needed to find his way down. A few more attempts and he would be forced to give up and return to his base. The sound of the engine changed, and suddenly there he was, skiing up to the dock out of nowhere.

"Come on; come on!" he yelled out his open window. We grabbed our gear and ran down the dock. Minutes later we were buckled in and on our way down the lake at full speed. But what were we speeding toward? "No problem," the pilot yelled to me—a notoriously poor flyer—over the roar of the engine. "See that spot of sun? That's all we need." Sure enough, I saw one tiny break in the fog. We flew toward the light, fog all around us, then broke through into a bright, clear fall day.

Below us, the whole lake was again covered in fog. Even our little light spot was gone, but we were safe. It looked like a good day for fishing.

From *Everyday Abundance*
BY TONI SORTOR

COMFORTING HANDS

*Praise be to the God and Father of our Lord Jesus Christ,
the Father of compassion and the God of all comfort.*

2 CORINTHIANS 1:3 NIV

Arla felt overwhelmed as she gazed at her mother's belongings. It had only been a few days since her mother passed away. Arla felt forsaken and lost. She sat wearily on a box in the garage and prayed for help through trembling lips. "I can't do this on my own, Lord," she whispered. . . .

She continued praying for a long time, the tears washing and cleansing her wounded heart. Finally, she stopped. A presence well known to Arla surrounded her: the comforting love of God.

Arla noticed the workbench. There lay her mother's gardening gloves and some small tools. Her mom often handed her a tool and showed how working the soil and flowers with her hands could be a good way of sorting out life's problems. Arla remembered them working alongside each other, sharing secrets and concerns, later taking them to God in prayer. God had touched her mom with a special gift of gardening and listening. . . .

She felt God's sweet comfort as she dug holes, planted bulbs, and dropped the seeds in place. Her thoughts cleared. Decisions Arla needed to make began falling into place. She knew she wasn't alone. She had the same wise, comforting God who had been with her mother and her all along.

From *When I'm in His Presence*
BY ANITA CORRINE DONIHUE

THE LORD'S YOKE

"Come to me, all you who are weary and burdened,
and I will give you rest.
Take my yoke upon you and learn from me,
for I am gentle and humble in heart,
and you will find rest for your souls.
For my yoke is easy and my burden is light."

MATTHEW 11:28–30 NIV

*N*ow that I have given You my all, Lord Jesus, Your yoke fits perfectly. Thank You for it and for teaching me gentleness and humility by wearing it. In doing so, I find peace and rest. You show me how we carry the loads together. This way I have twice the strength. All I need to do is follow and obey. You are the One who knows what is best.

No longer do I have to dig in stubbornly and claim my rights, because You go before me and fight those battles. Thank You, Lord, for giving me Your all. You could have called on Your angels to deliver You from the cross. Instead, You died a criminal's death. How could You have so much love?

I take up my cross and follow You, Lord. I know You help lighten the load as I trust completely in Your time, Your purpose, and Your way when troubles come. I will follow each day in Your footsteps. It doesn't matter where I stand: in poverty, wealth, fame, or glory. In everything, I will put You first and tell others about Your love.

From *When I'm Praising God*
BY ANITA CORRINE DONIHUE

I KNOW I BELONG TO GOD

O my Father, if it be possible,
let this cup pass from me:
nevertheless not as I will, but as thou wilt.

MATTHEW 26:39 KJV

*W*rap me in Your tender arms, I pray. Comfort and heal me. I trust You never to abandon me, even to the grave. You have promised to make Your path known to me. You, Lord, already have a plan for my future.

Thank You for allowing me to rest securely in You. Thank You for going before and behind me, for being on my right hand and left. You have told me there is a time for everything; there is a season for every activity under heaven. I realize there's a time to be born and a time to die. Through all this, I praise You for Your favor that lasts a lifetime—even a life eternal.

The flowers will appear on the earth once again, and the time of the singing of the birds will come. (See Song of Solomon 2:12 KJV.)

Thank You for helping me cling to You, my rock and my strength. Though I tremble, I shall not be destroyed. Though I shake, I shall not be removed from Your everlasting arms.

From *When God Calls Me Blessed*
BY ANITA CORRINE DONIHUE

BAKING COOKIES? BAH! HUMBUG!

*"Do not be afraid. I bring you good news of great joy
that will be for all the people.
Today in the town of David a Savior
has been born to you; he is Christ the Lord."*

LUKE 2:10–11 NIV

"This year, no cookie baking!" my eighty-year-old mom chided as we discussed holiday plans. I agreed.

Last year my daughter-in-law Robin decided to host a Christmas cookie-baking day. I looked forward to an entire day of mixing, baking, and decorating about as much as I welcomed a fly in my cookie mix. But in an attempt not to squelch Robin's youthful enthusiasm and holiday spirit, Mom and I agreed.

After hours of rolling, sifting, sprinkling, and stirring, the "older" ladies ambled to the living room.

"I'm exhausted," I said as I eased into a chair.

"I am, too," Mom replied, resting her head against the back of the couch. "You know, I just can't keep up like I used to."

"Hey, where'd you guys go?" Robin yelled through the house.

"Bah! Humbug! to the baking scene," I mumbled under my breath. But I kept my voice low, like a subdued Scrooge. "We're coming," I assured the girls with a sigh as Mom and I lifted our sagging bodies with simultaneous groans.

At the end of the day, I determined to simplify the holiday process in the future and concentrate on the real meaning of the season—the coming of Jesus Christ to this earth to redeem us from our sins.

From *Laughter Therapy*
BY TINA KRAUSE

DO I NEED TO KNOW THIS?

*Such knowledge is too wonderful for me,
too lofty for me to attain.*

PSALM 139:6 NIV

I have a theory that the human brain eventually gets full. The tighter you pack it, the more it will leak out old facts, especially as you get older. At least that seems to be my experience. For instance, now that we have grandchildren, it's less important for me to remember my children's names and more important to remember those of the grandchildren, so I have been known to call my son by my grandson's name, or my grandson is suddenly elevated to a son. Something's leaking, you see.

I've become highly selective in what I learn. I fish, but I don't take fish off the hook. That's something I don't need to know right now. I know how to use a computer but choose not to know how to attach files to an E-mail. Would you believe my husband wants me to learn how to balance the checkbook on the computer?

Where's the blessing in this state of affairs? Well, I've been blessed with a loving family that thinks it's funny when I forget their names. My refusal to learn every silly fact that comes by leaves me time to play with my grandchildren. I'm sure there's no scientific basis for my "full brain" theory, but it's not a subject I intend to research. It would take up precious room in my brain.

From *Everyday Abundance*
BY TONI SORTOR

CIRCLES OF LOVE

Let us. . .love. . .with actions and in truth.

1 JOHN 3:18 NIV

One hot day last summer, my seventy-five-year-old mother, my eleven-year-old daughter, and I walked together across a sun-baked lawn. My mother's heart was bothering her, and we walked very slowly, but my daughter didn't mind; she's been complaining that I walk too fast ever since she was small. I listened to their soft voices, watching the way their heads bent toward each other, and I was startled to realize that my daughter is taller than my mother now. My mother said something, and I heard my daughter laugh out loud with delight.

And at that moment, I was suddenly, completely happy. I didn't want to be anywhere but right there, with the young woman to whom I had given life, with the older woman who had given me life. I thought of another woman, my mother's mother, now in heaven, and I imagined a young woman who is yet to be born, my daughter's daughter. Together we form a chain, a chain of love reaching from the past into the future.

From *Just the Girls*
BY ELLYN SANNA

REALITY

The glory of young men is their strength,
gray hair the splendor of the old.

PROVERBS 20:29 NIV

*S*omeone made me have my picture taken today. I could have refused, but I was in a good mood (note the *was*), so I said I would do it. My husband got out his new digital camera, reread the directions, and in fifteen minutes the photo was on its way from our computer to theirs. Instant ugly.

The problem is, I really had to look at all the pictures to choose the best of the bunch. Usually I look at other things in our pictures—kids, dogs, cat, fish—never at myself. But there I was in close-up, every wrinkle showing, my hair flat, and my smile crooked. I don't deny that's how I usually look to the world—I'm not delusional—but that's not how I think I look. Inside, I'm still somewhere in middle age, so my mental picture is younger than the person in the photo. A lot younger. Thinner, too.

Even worse, I know there's not much chance that things will look better in the next picture. No matter how much I diet or exercise, those wrinkles are there to stay. So it's time to update my mental image, to admit I am the grandmother in the photo and be grateful that I've reached this age. I'm not young anymore, but God still loves me, and so do my family and friends.

From *Everyday Abundance*
BY TONI SORTOR

DRIVING CLASS

Let the wise listen and add to their learning,
and let the discerning get guidance.

PROVERBS 1:5 NIV

*F*or the next two days, I will be sitting in the public library taking a defensive driving class. I don't want to go. I've never had a ticket or accident in my life, and eight hours is a large chunk of time. I'm afraid I might fail the test.

It's not that I think this class is a bad idea. It's a good one—for all the other people on the road. The only time my driving ability is questionable is when I have to back up, and I go to great lengths to avoid doing that. Sometimes I get a little sleepy when driving long distances, too. My night vision is getting poor, but I rarely drive at night. Will stuff like that be covered, or will I have to learn—again—how to control my car in a spin (in an area where we have one or two inches of snow or ice a year)?

New experiences can be slightly frightening and irritating as we age. Things have gone well enough so far; why mess with success? What if I fail the test? Okay, I'll go, even though I don't need this class and will go bonkers sitting on a hard metal chair for eight hours. But what if I fail the test?

Update: There was no test!

From *Everyday Abundance*
BY TONI SORTOR

GRANDCHILDREN

Children's children are a crown to the aged.

PROVERBS 17:6 NIV

I loved it when our children were young. I've never been so tired or had as much fun. We all survived the teen years of growing separation, but there were some lonely years when they went their own ways. We would sometimes wish we had more children but knew we were too old to go through all that again. Then the Lord blessed us with grandchildren.

Suddenly we are wise again, loved just because we're there. I'm sure they feel we are a bit odd, and I occasionally catch them giving each other meaningful glances that seem to say, "They're old. We must be patient with them." Nevertheless, they listen to my husband's old stories with fresh ears, begging tales of what their mother did when she was young (especially when she misbehaved). Their little legs walk as slowly as our old legs, and their fresh eyes see things we have ignored for years. We borrow our grandchildren and spoil them rotten, leaving their parents to straighten them out when we return them full of junk food and thinking the world revolves around them.

Not only do we need our grandchildren, they need us, too. They need our unconditional love and approval. They need to feel they could never disappoint us. They need someone to pronounce them worthy and good, no matter what they do. They are our joy, our pleasure, our blessing in old age.

From *Everyday Abundance*
BY TONI SORTOR

HEALING THE HURTING HEART

Surely he took up our infirmities and carried our sorrows,
yet we considered him stricken by God,
smitten by him, and afflicted.
But he was pierced for our transgressions,
he was crushed for our iniquities;
the punishment that brought us peace was upon him,
and by his wounds we are healed.

ISAIAH 53:4–5 NIV

Thank You, Father, for healing my hurting heart. You took my turmoil and turned it into triumph. You gave me life anew with joy and made me whole.

Once my heart was crushed with grief. . . . I was so hurt I wanted to die. But I knew this was against all You had taught me.

I cried out to You for relief. You came. Your Spirit visited me and anointed me. You healed my broken heart and set me free from my emotional pain. You comforted me as I gave each injury of my soul to You. You forgave my sins and helped me to forgive others.

You anointed me with the oil of gladness and took away my mourning. You placed a garment of praise on my shoulders in place of a spirit of despair.

Through Your presence, Your Word, and Christian loved ones, You helped me rebuild my life into something good and victorious. You gave me back a zest for living. Thank You for planting my feet on Your solid rock. I praise You for using my heartaches and trials to teach me wisdom, empathy, and compassion.

From *When I'm Praising God*
BY ANITA CORRINE DONIHUE

A CLOSER WALK WITH THEE

And the angel of the LORD admonished Joshua, saying,
"Thus says the LORD of hosts,
'If you will walk in My ways
and if you will perform My service,
then you will also govern My house
and also have charge of My courts,
and I will grant you free access
among these who are standing here.' "

ZECHARIAH 3:6–7 NASB

*O*ur world has seemingly become obsessed with angelic beings. In addition to popular movies and a weekly television show starring "angels," items saturate the marketplace with supposed likenesses of the heavenly hosts. But such representations pale in comparison with an actual offer to walk among the angels.

God Himself is making such a conditional promise to Joshua, the High Priest. If he will "walk in God's ways," then the Lord will grant him free access to stroll through His heaven with these angelic beings.

As incredible an offer as this might have been for Joshua, an even more miraculous invitation awaits those who accept Jesus Christ as their Lord and Savior. For immediately they can enjoy the very presence of God every day of their lives. When we make a commitment to Him, His Spirit comes to indwell us. "However, you are not in the flesh but in the Spirit, if indeed the Spirit of God dwells in you. But if anyone does not have the Spirit of Christ, he does not belong to Him" (Romans 8:9 NASB).

From *Daily Wisdom for Women*
BY CAROL L. FITZPATRICK

SEALED BY THE HOLY SPIRIT

In Him, you also, after listening to the message of truth,
the gospel of your salvation—having also believed,
you were sealed in Him with the Holy Spirit of promise,
who is given as a pledge of our inheritance,
with a view to the redemption of God's own possession,
to the praise of His glory.

EPHESIANS 1:13–14 NASB

*O*rnamental sealing waxes and metal impressions were used in the past as both a security measure and a statement of authenticity, especially by royalty. The king's signet ring was pressed into the hot melted wax, leaving an indelible and unique impression. Paul was inspired to use this image to describe how we, as believers, are sealed by God's Holy Spirit.

The apostle Paul penned the Book of Ephesians between A.D. 60 to 62 while he was a prisoner in Rome. Ephesus, the fourth largest city in the Roman Empire, was steeped in idolatrous worship.

Into this spiritual darkness God sent Paul. The Lord desired to use this cultural setting to call out for Himself a church so that He could shine the light of truth upon this evil place.

From *Daily Wisdom for Women*
BY CAROL L. FITZPATRICK

THE FRUIT OF THE SPIRIT

But the fruit of the Spirit is
love, joy, peace, patience, kindness, goodness,
faithfulness, gentleness, self-control;
against such things there is no law.
Now those who belong to Christ Jesus have crucified the
flesh with its passions and desires.
If we live by the Spirit,
let us also walk by the Spirit.

GALATIANS 5:22–25 NASB

*W*hen we become Christians we receive spiritual gifts as a result of our inward relationship with Jesus Christ. These gifts are known in the Bible as the fruit of the Spirit, but what does that really mean?

Inventoried in today's Scripture are qualities that, apart from God's power, would likely not be displayed in our character.

Take, for instance, joy. How many truly joyful people do you know? Most of us could probably count them on one hand. Joy is the inward peace and sufficiency which transcends life's circumstances.

So, what's the catch? Why is God showering us with these gifts? Because they prove that He can enter a human life and affect her or him with change, that others might also be won to Christ as they observe this miracle.

From *Daily Wisdom for Women*
BY CAROL L. FITZPATRICK

MAPS

Each man has his own gift from God;
one has this gift, another has that.

1 CORINTHIANS 7:7 NIV

I admire my husband for many reasons, one of which is the fact that he never gets lost. He reads maps for the fun of it. Even though our chances of driving through Antarctica are slim, he will sit for an hour studying the topography of that frozen continent. If we ever get seriously turned around on the way south, he's ready.

I, on the other hand, have been known to forget the way home from the supermarket, especially if we've just moved. I can read a map if I pull over and stop, but I can't refold an open map, so I never pull over and stop. My dead reckoning is better than my husband's— I never get lost twice in the same place, and I can smell a fast-food restaurant two miles before the golden arches appear on the horizon. I give directions by saying, "Turn left after Joe's Diner"; he says, "Turn north 1.5 miles after the junction of Routes 1 and 287."

Between us we eventually reach most destinations; my way just takes longer. So the next time I find him memorizing a road map of Kent, England, I'll thank the Lord for my husband's attention to details and call the travel agent, knowing we won't get lost on the way to Canterbury.

From *Everyday Abundance*
BY TONI SORTOR

MEEK AND LOWLY

Take my yoke upon you, and learn of me;
for I am meek and lowly in heart:
and ye shall find rest unto your souls.

MATTHEW 11:29 KJV

*W*hat can be more delicious to a delicate self-love than to hear itself applauded for having none! The truly meek and lowly heart does not want to talk about its *me* at all, either for good or evil. It wants to forget its very existence. As Fenelon writes, it says to this *me,* "I do not know you and am not interested in you. You are a stranger to me, and I do not care what happens to you nor how you are treated." If people slight you or treat you with contempt or neglect, the meek and lowly heart accepts all as its rightful portion. True humility makes us love to be treated, both by God and man, as we feel our imperfections really deserve; and, instead of resenting such treatment, we welcome it and are thankful for it. I remember being greatly struck by a saying of Madame Guyon's, that she had learned to give thanks for every mortification that befell her, because she had found mortifications so helpful in putting self to death. . . . Humiliations are the medicine that the Great Physician generally administers to cure the spiritual dropsy caused by feeding the soul on continual thoughts of *me.*

HANNAH WHITALL SMITH
From *A Gentle Spirit*
COMPILED BY ASHLEIGH BRYCE CLAYTON

CHRISTMAS JOY

And we have seen and testify
and proclaim to you the eternal life,
which was with the Father and was manifested to us—
what we have seen and heard we proclaim to you also,
so that you too may have fellowship with us;
and indeed our fellowship is with the Father,
and with His Son Jesus Christ.

1 JOHN 1:2–3 NASB

The countdown to Christmas has begun. Are your cards in the mail yet? What message have you extended to friends and family? Illustrations of cats in floppy red Santa caps or snowy winter scenes cannot effect a change in the lives of those who do not know the Christ of Christmas. For only the Word of God has the power to reach into searching hearts and bring hope.

Where will you find joy this Christmas? It's not in brightly colored packages under the tree. And unless your loved ones know the Lord, jubilation probably won't be present at your family gatherings, either. For we cannot partake of this commodity apart from Christ.

Consider today what printed message you will send to loved ones this Christmas. . .a message of hope about Christ the Savior, or a scene in which He is nowhere to be found?

From *Daily Wisdom for Women*
BY CAROL L. FITZPATRICK

GOOD NEWS OF GREAT JOY

"This will be a sign to you:
You will find a baby wrapped in cloths
and lying in a manger."

LUKE 2:12 NIV

*I*t was December 24, and half the town was standing in the checkout lines at Shop Rite, fully three-quarters of us in foul moods. Why couldn't people plan ahead? What was that woman going to do with five pounds of broccoli? All I had in my basket were five sweet potatoes, for which I would stand in line at least ten minutes. Bah, humbug!

Ahead of me, a tiny baby reclined in his carrier, which was wedged into the metal seat meant for toddlers and eggs. He was so bundled up his cheeks glowed red. When his eyes met mine, he broke into a full-body smile, his arms reaching vaguely in my direction, his feet thrashing merrily, his mouth making little baby gurgles.

"He's so beautiful," I told his mother as I smiled back at the baby, which threw him into even more ecstatic wiggles.

In seconds people from neighboring lines were playing peek-aboo, smiling at those near them, totally captivated by the baby's complete and unconditional happiness. Suddenly I knew exactly how the shepherds and wise men must have felt so long ago. "Merry Christmas," I said to the cashier as I reached her.

"Merry Christmas to you," she replied, still grinning in the baby's direction as his mother made her way toward the exit. "Cash or charge?"

From *Everyday Abundance*
BY TONI SORTOR

IF YOU WANT JOY

Thou wilt shew me the path of life:
in thy presence is fulness of joy;
at thy right hand there are pleasures for evermore.

PSALM 16:11 KJV

Just as the simple presence of the mother makes the child's joy, so does the simple fact of God's presence make our joy. The mother may not make a single promise to the child, nor explain any of her plans or purposes, but she is, and that is enough for the child. And to the child, there is behind all that changes and can change the one unchangeable joy of mother's existence. While the mother lives, the child will be cared for; and the child knows this, instinctively, if not intelligently, and rejoices in knowing it. And to the children of God, as well, there is behind all that changes and can change the one unchangeable joy that God is. And while He is, His children will be cared for, and they ought to know it and rejoice in it, as instinctively and far more intelligently than the child of human parents. For what else can God do, being what He is? Neglect, indifference, forgetfulness, ignorance, are all impossible to Him. He knows everything, He cares about everything, He can manage everything, and He loves us! Surely this is enough for a "fullness of joy" beyond the power of words to express; no matter what else may be missed besides.

HANNAH WHITALL SMITH
From *A Gentle Spirit*
COMPILED BY ASHLEIGH BRYCE CLAYTON

ROYAL BLUE PERFORMANCE

The LORD is good to all;
he has compassion on all he has made.

PSALM 145:9 NIV

The day was like any other. The time, early afternoon. Bob and I had driven to a routine doctor's appointment for me about ten miles from our home. As usual, we were exceptionally busy and wanted a little extra time together. Taking the old river road home seemed a nice way to gear down.

Sun rays splintered through the clouds and reflected off a soft haze hovering over the river. Bob and I drank in the tranquility.

As we rounded a bend, a four-foot blue heron stood elegantly by the roadside. We slowed to a near stop. The royal-colored bird spread its huge wings and gracefully glided above the river. It maneuvered itself to fly parallel with our car windows. Soon the huge bird must have spotted a fish. Its trim body angled perfectly, and it dove out of sight.

We were exhilarated and felt the hectic-laden tension slip from our bodies. The entertainment from a magnificent blue heron surpassed anything we had witnessed for a long time.

Bob and I still talk about the river drive and the lovely blue heron. For years we had tried to simply get a glimpse of one through our binoculars in a local protected nesting area. Instead, God chose to bless us that day with a front-row (car) seat, full-view personal performance.

From *When I'm in His Presence*
BY ANITA CORRINE DONIHUE

WHO ARE THE FAITHFUL?

Help, LORD, for the godly man ceases to be,
For the faithful disappear from among the sons of men.
They speak falsehood to one another;
With flattering lips and with a double heart they speak.

PSALM 12:1–2 NASB

*W*ho are the faithful? They are the ones who continue to follow God, no matter what obstacles are thrown in their path. One of the faithful, a dear friend who has debilitating multiple sclerosis, is one of the most joyful Christians I know. Jo must be assisted to the podium, but once seated on a wooden stool the weakness in her legs is forgotten. The songs which emanate from her wondrous spirit are a radiant tribute to her Savior, Jesus Christ.

Another friend, Sue, has led a Bible study for years, despite the fact that her husband is frequently out of work and their finances are at times nearly nonexistent. She continues at her post, knowing that God is not out of resources. And each time their family stands on the brink of impending disaster, God rescues them.

By now you have probably decided that it doesn't pay to become one of my friends. But I must reassure you that neither of these women considers shrinking back from following Christ. Instead, they agree with the apostle Paul that these present circumstances and trials are but "light and momentary" compared with the peace we will have in Christ for all eternity.

From *Daily Wisdom for Women*
BY CAROL L. FITZPATRICK

THE LORD'S FRIENDSHIP

"I am the true vine, and My Father is the vinedresser.
Abide in Me, and I in you.
As the Father loved Me, I also have loved you;
abide in My love."

JOHN 15:1, 4, 9 NKJV

Here I am, Lord, after the late shift. Work was hard, fast, and stressful. I'm tired, but my body is so tense I can't sleep. All I can think of is the quiet peace You give me. Thank You, God, for meeting me here in my weariness and for Your friendship.

Your sweet presence fills the air. A feeling of expectancy greets me, as though You have been waiting for me to share my work events with You. I sense You listening intently to my every concern. The victories, the crises, even the funny happenings. I also bring my coworkers to You in prayer.

Like a new chapter in a book, I feel You speak to me. You comfort and assure me of answers to my prayers.

Thank You for my loved ones sleeping in nearby rooms. Their soft, steady breathing sounds so good. I ask Your blessings on each one and thank You for keeping them safe.

My eyelids grow heavy; I find it difficult to form my thoughts on You.

"Rest, my beloved," I feel You say.

Thank You, Lord, for meeting me here again and being my dearest Friend.

From *When I'm in His Presence*
BY ANITA CORRINE DONIHUE

EMBRACING THE WORD

"I have come that they may have life,
and have it to the full."

JOHN 10:10 NIV

*J*esus doesn't want you to have a pinched, skinny little life, a life that's constricted by doubts and fears about your own worth. No, He wants you to have a life that's full and rich. That's what this Bible verse from the Gospel of John is saying: Jesus wants you to really live. The King James Version of the Bible calls the same concept "abundant" life. In the Gospel of Luke, Jesus says that "a good measure, pressed down, shaken together and running over, will be poured into your lap" (6:38 NIV).

This isn't the way the world pictures the Christian life. People who don't know Christ tend to think that the life He offers is one that's full of legalistic rules and restrictions. But instead, Jesus loves you so much that He came to earth and died—so that through Him, you could have a real life, a full life—forever.

Jesus is reaching out to you today with the same compassionate love. He wants to heal your wounded self-esteem. You are precious to Him. When you give your identity to Him, He will give you back more than you can ever imagine. He wants to free you from all your doubts about your own worth. He wants you to live life to its full.

From *Created for a Purpose*
BY DARLENE SALA

GOD CARES

Therefore take no thought, saying,
What shall we eat? or, What shall we drink? or,
Wherewithal shall we be clothed?
. . .for your heavenly Father knoweth that
ye have need of all these things."

MATTHEW 6:31–32 KJV

Who is the best cared for in every household? Is it not the little children? And does not the least of all, the helpless baby, receive the largest share? We all know that the baby toils not, neither does it spin; and yet it is fed, and clothed, and loved, and rejoiced in more tenderly than the hardest worker of them all.

This life of faith, then, consists in just this—being a child in the Father's house. And when this is said, enough is said to transform every weary, burdened life into one of blessedness and rest.

Let the ways of childish confidence and freedom from care, which so please you and win your heart in your own little ones, teach you what should be your ways with God; and, leaving yourself in His hands, learn to be literally "careful for nothing"; and you shall find it to be a fact that the peace of God, which passeth all understanding, shall keep (as with a garrison) your heart and mind through Christ Jesus.

HANNAH WHITALL SMITH
From *A Gentle Spirit*
COMPILED BY ASHLEIGH BRYCE CLAYTON

HOW TO ENTER IN

And thy Father which seeth in secret
shall reward thee openly.

MATTHEW 6:6 KJV

A Christian lady who had this feeling was once expressing to a friend how impossible she found it to say, "Thy will be done," and how afraid she should be to do it. She was the mother of an only little boy who was the heir to a great fortune and the idol of her heart. After she had stated her difficulties fully, her friend said, "Suppose your little Charley should come running to you tomorrow and say, 'Mother, I am always going to obey you, and I will trust your love.' How would you feel towards him? Would you say to yourself, 'Ah, now I shall have a chance to make Charley miserable. I will take away all his pleasures and fill his life with every hard and disagreeable thing that I can find. I will compel him to do just the things that are the most difficult for him to do and will give him all sorts of impossible commands.'" "Oh, no, no, no!" exclaimed the indignant mother. "You know I would not. You know I would hug him to my heart and cover him with kisses and would hasten to fill his life with all that was sweetest and best." "And are you more tender and more loving than God?"

HANNAH WHITALL SMITH
From *A Gentle Spirit*
COMPILED BY ASHLEIGH BRYCE CLAYTON

I LOVE THE LORD BEST

I will never leave thee, nor forsake thee.
So that we may boldly say,
The Lord is my helper, and I will not fear.

HEBREWS 13:5–6 KJV

I love to have You near me, Lord. I feel secure and loved in Your presence, like a child nestled in its mother's arms.

I sense Your pride for me in my accomplishments. How I treasure Your listening to me when I fail or when things go wrong. I feel Your comfort. When I grieve, I nestle within the surroundings of Your Holy Spirit and soak up Your warmth and love.

In life's celebrations, You rejoice with me; in life's challenges, You urge me on. In life's discouragements, You encourage. In the storms, You calm my fears. In my insecurities, You remind me of how much You treasure me. In victories, You are jubilant. In defeats, You are closer than ever.

You know my very being. You see my attitude, my desires, my fears, my weariness, and even my illnesses before I recognize them. How wonderful is the way You strengthen me.

Thank You for being my Good Shepherd, for nourishing and caring for me spiritually, mentally, and physically. I thank You for guiding me into safe areas and for leading me to Your living water.

You are my past, my present, my future, my life, my all.

From *When I'm Praising God*
BY ANITA CORRINE DONIHUE

GOD IS REAL

*Now faith is the substance of things hoped for,
the evidence of things not seen.*

HEBREWS 11:1 KJV

*B*ecause God is not visibly present to the eye, it is difficult to feel that a transaction with Him is real. I suppose that if, when we made our acts of consecration, we could actually see Him present with us, we should feel it to be a very real thing and would realize that we had given our word to Him and could not dare to take it back, no matter how much we might wish to do so. Such a transaction would have to us the binding power that a spoken promise to an earthly friend always has to a man of honor. What we need, therefore, is to see that God's presence is a certain fact always, and that every act of our soul is done before Him, and that a word spoken in prayer is as really spoken to Him as if our eyes could see Him and our hands could touch Him. Then we shall cease to have such vague conceptions of our relations with Him and shall feel the binding force of every word we say in His presence.

HANNAH WHITALL SMITH
From *A Gentle Spirit*
COMPILED BY ASHLEIGH BRYCE CLAYTON

TRUE LOVE MEANS SACRIFICE

They spat on Him,
and took the reed and began to beat Him on the head.
After they had mocked Him,
they took the scarlet robe off Him
and put His own garments back on Him,
and led Him away to crucify Him.

MATTHEW 27:30–31 NASB

Years ago the popular movie *Love Story* coined the unforgettable phrase, "Love means never having to say you're sorry." What a fallacy, and more is the pity for those who bought into this lie!

For love demands that we always say we're sorry. How else can relationships be restored?

Those two words, "I'm sorry," have the power to keep families and churches together. I once knew a pastor whose refusal to recognize his humanity caused almost half of the church family to seek membership elsewhere. In his eyes he had done nothing wrong, but what harm would have been done to admit the possibility of poor judgment?

To admit fallibility is to make a sacrifice. To have done nothing wrong and to offer the ultimate sacrifice is an act only possible by God's Son. Jesus' offering of His body at Calvary gave eternal life to all who believe in Him.

Is there someone from whom you are estranged who is waiting to hear those two little words? Say you're sorry.

From *Daily Wisdom for Women*
BY CAROL L. FITZPATRICK

WHO IS OUR FIRST LOVE?

Do not be yoked together with unbelievers.

2 CORINTHIANS 6:14 NIV

How can we possibly love God more than our sweethearts or spouses, our children or parents? These people are more precious to us than priceless jewels. Still, this is what God calls us to do as Christians.

Obviously, our love for one another is incredibly strong. Many a story is told about boundless acts of sacrifice shown for loved ones and even to strangers. This love, no matter how strong, is human and sometimes fragile. Even in the best of circumstances, human love errs. Unkind words may be spoken. Thoughtless actions can cut to the heart. The fire of human love may become vulnerable enough to flicker, fade, or even die. We have heard many times of strong affection turning to intense bitterness.

How does God's love differ? It is unselfish, perfect, and pure. It doesn't manipulate or expect a payback. We can thank Him over and over that we are able to count on His care every day, in every circumstance. God's holy compassion cleanses us from selfishness and wrong. When we put Him first, the Lord teaches us to cherish one another more with a deep, unselfish, measureless love.

He cherishes us in spite of our failures and appreciates our efforts to serve and obey Him. How awesome and farseeing our Lord is! His example of pure, undefiled compassion helps us to look beyond the imperfections in others, appreciate them, and give them the love of God.

From *When I Hear His Call*
BY ANITA CORRINE DONIHUE

DESTINATION UNKNOWN

Come unto me, all ye that labour and are heavy laden,
and I will give you rest.

MATTHEW 11:28 KJV

A Sunday afternoon all to ourselves? Bob and I couldn't believe it.

"Get in the car," he gently prodded.

I had learned after thirty-eight years of marriage that I had a husband who was filled with romantic surprises. . . .

We drove and drove through beautiful countryside. . . .

We happily chatted about recent events. We were so caught up in the moment that we missed the turn to return home.

We glanced at each other with adventurous looks. "Let's keep going," we both said at once.

After hours of driving we came to a forest fire and watched the helicopters smother it. We kept driving and passed deer, leisurely munching grass by the side of the road.

Soon we arrived in a small town on the other side of the pass. We had no luggage, toiletries, or changes of clothing. It didn't discourage us. We stopped for the essentials at a nearby grocery store.

We checked into a motel and called our oldest son, so no one would think we had disappeared forever. A relaxing night was spent talking and reading.

The next morning we returned home well rested. We both found we had added another very special memory to our married lives.

I'm thankful for God's plan for relaxation and for my loving husband who knows when we need a break.

From *When I'm Praising God*
BY ANITA CORRINE DONIHUE

A HUSBAND'S LOVE

Wives, be subject to your own husbands, as to the Lord.
For the husband is the head of the wife,
as Christ also is the head of the church,
He Himself being the Savior of the body.
But as the church is subject to Christ,
so also the wives ought to be
to their husbands in everything.

EPHESIANS 5:22–24 NASB

*W*ives, our role is that of a helpmate, not doormat. It's critical to remember that God intended marriage to be a partnership. Thus, if each person vies for control, the union begins eroding until it simply dissolves. Instead, we need to build one another up.

"So husbands ought also to love their own wives as their own bodies. He who loves his own wife loves himself; for no one ever hated his own flesh, but nourishes and cherishes it, just as Christ also does the church, because we are members of His body" (Ephesians 5:28–29 NASB). If men truly loved their wives to this degree, there probably isn't a woman alive who'd run from it.

So what can we do to make things better? Pray. . .every single day. But especially when things are out of kilter. Know that God is vitally interested in the success of your marriage and act accordingly.

From *Daily Wisdom for Women*
BY CAROL L. FITZPATRICK

LOVING OUR MATES

So husbands ought to love their own wives
as their own bodies;
he who loves his wife loves himself.

EPHESIANS 5:28 NKJV

*O*ur son Jonathan and daughter-in-law Cynthia have an abiding love for each other that will last a lifetime. It gives my husband Bob and me warm feelings each time we hear them talk about one another.

Recently, Jonathan called just to say hello. He told how when Cynthia curled up near him, he discovered a gray hair in her head. They were so excited, they jerked it out and held it up to the light, marveling over its silvery sheen. They carefully placed the silver strand in a plastic baggie for safekeeping.

Bob and I chuckled. He warned them not to jerk out too many, or she might grow bald. Jonathan visualized how beautiful his dear wife would be years from now with a head adorned in silvery gray.

He pictured how they would take walks in the moonlight, the same as they do now. In his vision, his wife's silvery hair reflected the light of the moon, their love being as strong as ever. (I believe it will be even stronger.)

The Bible says God knows every hair on our heads. Isn't it incredible that He loves us every hour of every day? It's even more incredible that His love will remain with us forever.

From *When I Hear His Call*
BY ANITA CORRINE DONIHUE

I THANK GOD FOR THE MAN I LOVE

And now these three remain:
faith, hope and love.
But the greatest of these is love.

1 CORINTHIANS 13:13 NIV

*H*e gazes at me from across the packed room. We're at just another meeting, but I dressed to look my best. Do I see the same twinkle in his eyes I saw when we first met? Do I see the same look he wore on our wedding day? Am I so blessed that he still gazes at me with the same love and pride? Thank You, Lord, for that look. Thank You for today and for him.

Help me show to him the same love and thoughtfulness as when we first married. In our hurried schedules, let us look for time to spend with each other. Sometimes I love even sharing a second glass of iced tea on the patio at sundown.

I think of changes we've faced and will continue to experience. We have fallen in love with each other over and over again, even while changing.

Teach us to keep respecting one another's feelings. Teach us to put each other first, after You.

And, Lord, help me keep myself in a way that he will always look across the room with love and pride.

From *When I'm on My Knees*
BY ANITA CORRINE DONIHUE

WE DO

"A man must leave his father and mother when he marries,
so that he can be perfectly joined to his wife,
and the two shall be one."

EPHESIANS 5:31 TLB

The church was packed with friends as the simple ceremony began.

Bob and I gazed into each other's love-struck eyes as Pastor Jerry led us through our vows. Two of our sons presented us with our rings.

Pastor Jerry reminded us of the sanctity of marriage. Then came the part, "Who gives this woman to be married to this man?"

A deep, reverent "We do" chorused from my father and our four grown sons. We paused and prayed, thanking God for the lifetime of marriage and family He has given us.

Forty years, and we love each other more than ever. He still looks at me with a sparkle in his eyes. He opens doors for me and buys me flowers. My heart still goes pitter-patter when he enters a room. When we go somewhere together, I still dress to look my best for my sweetheart and friend.

Our anniversary was more than a celebration of forty years of marriage. It was a celebration of life in Jesus Christ with the ones we love the most: each other, our sons, our daughters-in-love, our grandchildren, our parents, our family of God. Most of all, we celebrated our love for the Lord, the Author and Finisher of it all.

From *When God Sees Me Through*
BY ANITA CORRINE DONIHUE

SOUL FOOD

Wherefore do ye spend money
for that which is not bread?
and your labour for that which satisfieth not?
hearken diligently unto me,
and eat ye that which is good,
and let your soul delight itself in fatness.

ISAIAH 55:2 KJV

*G*ive us this day our daily bread" is a prayer that includes the soul as well as the body, and unless the religion of Christ contains this necessary food for our weekday lives, as well as for our Sunday lives, it is a grievous failure. But this it does. It is full of principles that fit into human life, as it is in its ordinary commonplace aspects; and the soul that would grow strong must feed itself on these, as well as on the more dainty fare of sermons and services and weekly celebrations.

Does not plain common sense teach us that when people feed their souls upon a diet of gossip or of frivolities of any kind, they must necessarily suffer from languor of spiritual life, debility of spiritual digestion, failure of vitality, and a creeping moral paralysis?

"But lusted exceedingly in the wilderness, and tempted God in the desert. And he gave them their request; but sent leanness into their soul" (Psalm 106:14–15 KJV).

"Leanness of soul" arises far more often than we think from the indigestible nature of the spiritual food we have been feeding upon.

HANNAH WHITALL SMITH
From *A Gentle Spirit*
COMPILED BY ASHLEIGH BRYCE CLAYTON

BABES IN CHRIST

Therefore, putting aside all malice and all deceit and
hypocrisy and envy and all slander,
like newborn babies, long for the pure milk of the word,
so that by it you may grow in respect to salvation,
if you have tasted the kindness of the Lord.

1 PETER 2:1–3 NASB

*W*hen you have a new baby, you're starting with a clean slate. And although babies have inherited Adam's bent toward sinning, they haven't as yet exercised this "family affliction."

If we grow physically but ignore our spiritual needs, the potential for becoming a well-rounded human being is severely diminished, if not permanently stunted. This is the issue which Peter addresses in this passage. As mothers, grandmothers, step-mothers, and aunts, we have a God-ordained call to teach children the Word of God that they might someday enter the kingdom of God. Jesus said: "Whoever causes one of these little ones who believe in Me to stumble, it would be better for him to have a heavy millstone hung around his neck, and to be drowned in the depth of the sea" (Matthew 18:6 NASB).

That's pretty strong language. But look at the stakes! A child's whole life can be altered by someone who turns them away purposely from the truth of Jesus Christ.

From *Daily Wisdom for Women*
BY CAROL L. FITZPATRICK

THE GIFT OF LIFE

From birth I have relied on you;
you brought me forth from
my mother's womb.
I will ever praise you.

PSALM 71:6 NIV

*Y*ou would think that this was my first pregnancy, not my fourth; I am filled with such a sense of excitement and anticipation. Everything feels so new. Every kick and prod, every roll and tumble that this child delivers, fills me with awe. I am consumed with the yearning to hold and cuddle, to nurture, to bring this little person into a family eagerly awaiting the opportunity to love someone new.

Even with three more months of waiting, I am almost obsessed with thoughts of being ready. I am absurdly giddy over recent purchases—bottles, burp cloths, diapers. Friends watch and smile and shake their heads. "She's done all this before, what's the big deal?"

I'm not quite sure. Maybe I'm cherishing this experience so much because I know the pain of losing a life. Maybe it's the realization that I'm not getting any younger, and this may be our last child.

Whatever the reason, through it all—the discomfort, the nausea, the sickness, the aches and pains—I am always aware of the miracle growing within me. I praise my Creator for the gift of motherhood—and for the privilege and honor of serving Him in this way.

From *Time Out*
BY LEIGH ANN THOMAS

REFLECTED LOVE

*"By this all men will know
that you are my disciples,
if you love one another."*

JOHN 13:35 NIV

*B*ecause God's love is reflected in ours, our children will learn about God simply through motherhood's love. Oh, we need to teach our children about God and His Word. We need to read them Bible stories and pray with them, answer their questions, and take them to church. We need to live in such a way that they'll see what it means to be a Christian. But on much more basic level, they'll understand about a God who always hears, because when they were babies we responded to their cries. They'll be able to have faith in a God who meets their needs, because we saw that they never went hungry. God's strength and tenderness will be real to them because they caught a glimpse of it in our love, from the time they were born.

So, mothers, never let the world tell you that what you do is not important. Remember, when you rock your babies and sing a lullaby, your arms and voice are God's. When you do load after load of dirty diapers, and then grass-stained play clothes, and finally school clothes smeared with ketchup and chocolate pudding, remember, your hands are God's hands. And when you love your children unconditionally, all the way from colic to adolescent rebellion, you are loving with God's love. Through you, He will imprint Himself on your children's hearts.

From *A Mother's Love Is Forever*
BY ELLYN SANNA

OUR CHILDREN

These commandments that I give you today
are to be upon your hearts.
Impress them on your children.
Talk about them when you sit at home
and when you walk along the road,
when you lie down and when you get up.
Tie them as symbols on your hands
and bind them on your foreheads.
Write them on the doorframes of
your houses and on your gates.

DEUTERONOMY 6:6–9 NIV

The house rumbles with laughter and tussles. I hurry to keep up with it all. They are a heritage that comes from You. These bursts of energy in various sizes and personalities are like arrows in a warrior's hands.

I call on You for wisdom. Each day I thank You for guidance in handling different situations. Thank You, Lord, for how You help me teach our children about Your love. I treasure Your leading as I share Your lessons with them while we go about our activities at home, when we share walks, as we pray together at bedtime, and rise each morning to face a new day.

My husband and I have dedicated our lives and these children to You, Lord. I know for sure Your hand is and will be upon them throughout their entire lives.

I write Your words on plaques, pictures, and on our doorposts that, "As for me and my household, we will serve the LORD" (Joshua 24:15 NIV).

From *When I'm Praising God*
BY ANITA CORRINE DONIHUE

OUR NEWBORN BABY

> " *'The LORD bless you*
> *and keep you;*
> *the LORD make his face shine upon you*
> *and be gracious to you;*
> *the LORD turn his face toward you*
> *and give you peace.'* "

NUMBERS 6:24–26 NIV

*L*ook at our beautiful baby, Lord, at these tiny fingers wrapped around mine. Look how this darling rests securely in my arms. See Daddy's proud gaze. Already my heart overflows with love. I talked to and prayed for this sweet one even while the baby was still in my womb.

Today, O Lord, I dedicate our baby as a love offering to You. Like Hannah in days of old, I thank You for giving our little one to us. Here and now, I present our child at Your altar to be raised for Your service.

Let Your angels encamp around and about and protect from evil and harm. Help us teach Your ways by truth and example. I pray that You will create a special hunger in this little heart to know, love, and serve You completely.

Help me remember our child is lent to us for a little while and that You are the lender. Let me not take our dear one back from You or pursue my own ways outside Your will.

I will bless Your name, O Lord, thanking You for this wonderful infant gift. I praise Your name in my thoughts, motives, and actions forever.

From *When I'm on My Knees*
BY ANITA CORRINE DONIHUE

TEACH ME TO PARENT

Teach [God's commandments] to your children.

DEUTERONOMY 11:19 NIV

Thank You for my children, Lord. They are my most precious gifts from You. I look at them and see how they reflect different family members—their hair, their eyes, the little dimple like mine. Most of all, I pray they will have Your eyes and learn the wonders of Your ways.

Help me teach my children the lessons in Your Word. Remind me to talk about Your Scriptures in our home. May this become a way of life. Through the years, I pray my dear ones will learn to apply Your lessons to all they do.

When I must discipline, grant me love, strength, and consistency. Let me lead them into a life of love, responsibility, truth, and hope for the future. Grant me understanding as I work with each child, so I won't be too strict nor too lenient. Help me develop love and security in them, rather than fear and anger. Let everything I do be out of loving action, not reaction.

I can't think of a job more challenging than meeting the needs of my children. I can only do it through You, my Lord. Go before me, I pray. As I endeavor to do Your will, I petition Your help. Enable me to train up my children in the way they should go, so when they are older they will remain close to You. In Jesus' name I pray, Amen.

From *When God Sees Me Through*
BY ANITA CORRINE DONIHUE

THE VOCATION OF MATERNITY

Charm is deceptive, and beauty is fleeting;
but a woman who fears the LORD is to be praised.

PROVERBS 31:30 NIV

The best convent," I said, "for a woman is the seclusion of her own home. There she may find her vocation and fight her battles, and there she may learn the reality and the earnestness of life."

"Pshaw!" cried she. "Excuse me, however, for saying that; but some of the most brilliant girls I know have settled down into mere married women and spend their whole time nursing babies! Think how belittling!"

"Is it more so than spending it dressing, driving, dancing, and the like?"

"Of course it is. I had a friend once who shone like a star in society. She married and had four children as fast as she could. Well! What was the consequence? She lost her beauty, her spirit and animation, lost her youth, and lost her health. The only earthly things she can talk about are teething, dieting, and measles!"

I laughed at this exaggeration. . . . "As you have spoken plainly to me, knowing me to be a wife and mother, you must allow me to speak plainly in return," I began. "You will permit me to say that when you speak contemptuously of the vocation of maternity, you dishonor not only the mother who bore you but the Lord Jesus Himself, who chose to be born of woman and to be ministered unto by her through a helpless infancy."

From *Stepping Heavenward*
BY ELIZABETH PRENTISS

WEAK BUT WILLING

He has showed you, O man, what is good.
And what does the LORD require of you?
To act justly and to love mercy
and to walk humbly with your God.

MICAH 6:8 NIV

*I*t wasn't long after Dave earned his college degree that he felt God's call to the ministry. For the next several months Dave studied the Scriptures and asked God to help and lead him. The closer he drew to God through prayer and reading his Bible, the more he became aware of his weaknesses.

One morning Dave sat at the open kitchen window, deep in thought. Birds chirping caused him to glance outside at the bird feeder. He noticed one feathered creature singing more beautifully than the others. The little bird enthusiastically puffed out its chest, and glorious melodies filled the air. Dave was surprised when he discovered the bird had a missing leg. Still, it shuffled about, appeared happy, and kept singing. Serendipity? Or was this God answering his prayer? Dave believed it was the latter.

"God, You have promised me in Your Bible that Your grace is sufficient for me, and Your power is made perfect in my weakness. I trust You will provide me with confidence, joy, and strength."

In spite of Dave's weaknesses, God honored his faith. Doors opened for Dave to become a youth minister, where he is still winning souls for the Lord.

From *When God Calls Me Blessed*
BY ANITA CORRINE DONIHUE

AGAINST THE CURRENT

So likewise, whosoever he be of you
that forsaketh not all that he hath,
he cannot be my disciple.

LUKE 14:33 KJV

You must remember that our God has all knowledge and all wisdom, and that therefore it is very possible He may guide you into paths wherein He knows great blessings are awaiting you, but which, to the shortsighted human eyes around you, seem sure to result in confusion and loss. You must recognize the fact that God's thoughts are not as man's thoughts, nor His ways as man's ways; and that He alone, who knows the end of things from the beginning, can judge of what the results of any course of action may be. You must, therefore, realize that His very love for you may perhaps lead you to run counter to the loving wishes of even your dearest friends. You must learn that in order to be a disciple and follower of your Lord, you may be called upon to forsake inwardly all that you have. Unless the possibility of this is clearly recognized, you will be very likely to get into difficulty, because it often happens that the child of God who enters upon this life of obedience is sooner or later led into paths which meet with the disapproval of those he best loves; and unless he is prepared for this, and can trust the Lord through it all, he will scarcely know what to do.

HANNAH WHITALL SMITH
From *A Gentle Spirit*
COMPILED BY ASHLEIGH BRYCE CLAYTON

DRAWN TO OBEY

For it is God which worketh in you
both to will and to do of his good pleasure.

PHILIPPIANS 2:13 KJV

God's promise is that He will work in us to will as well as to do of His good pleasure. This means, of course, that He will take possession of our will and work it for us; and that His suggestions will come to us, not so much commands from the outside as desires springing up within. They will originate in our will; we shall feel as though we desired to do so and so, not as though we must. And this makes it a service of perfect liberty; for it is always easy to do what we desire to do, let the accompanying circumstances be as difficult as they may. Every mother knows that she could secure perfect and easy obedience in her child if she could only get into that child's will and work it for him, making him want himself to do the things she willed he should. And this is what our Father, in the new dispensation, does for His children; He "writes his laws on our hearts and on our minds," so that our affection and our understanding embrace them, and we are drawn to obey instead of being driven to it.

HANNAH WHITALL SMITH
From *A Gentle Spirit*
COMPILED BY ASHLEIGH BRYCE CLAYTON

A CALL TO HOLINESS

*"When you enter the land which
the LORD your God gives you,
you shall not learn to imitate
the detestable things of those nations.
There shall not be found among you. . .
one who practices witchcraft, or one who interprets omens,
or a sorcerer, or one who casts a spell, or a medium,
or a spiritist, or one who calls up the dead.
For whoever does these things is detestable to the LORD."*

DEUTERONOMY 18:9–12 NASB

*O*ur two sons easily tire of most board games. But they became immediately fascinated after one of their friends introduced them to the role-playing game Dungeons and Dragons. While our older son got a part-time job, which severely limited his free time, his younger brother went deeper and deeper into this seductive game.

About the same time, our church encouraged adults and high schoolers to sign up for the seminar "Basic Youth Conflicts." By the time the concluding all-day Saturday session rolled around, each one of us had been convicted by the Holy Spirit concerning our own "pet sins." All the way home that last evening our younger son spoke about how the game had usurped the time he used to spend with the Lord. He'd even begun feeling a strange sense of power come over him.

We watched as he pulled out a metal trash can and burned every one of the game's expensive books. From that moment Jeff never looked back.

Is God receiving all the glory in your life?

From *Daily Wisdom for Women*
BY CAROL L. FITZPATRICK

JUST GO

They that go. . .that do. . .
These see the works of the LORD,
and his wonders.

PSALM 107:23–24 KJV

Elijah had come far by following God's word. The word of the true, living God had never yet failed him, and so he went to a destitute widow in Zarephath, and he candidly spoke all the words God put into his mouth.

God was faithful, as He always is. The widow, her son, and Elijah ate for as long as the famine continued.

Elijah went. Elijah did. Elijah saw.

If, after awhile, I hear a word from the Lord, I, too, will get up and go where He leads me, do what He directs me to do. Then I will surely come again with rejoicing. Constantly, I am realizing God's wonderful provision for my every need and the desires of my heart, as I do His will. Perhaps, by being obedient, I will be used to encourage others in yielding to Him, too.

I may at first think that this new way cannot possibly work. When I get set in my old way, my own way, that seems to be the only viable option. But God's ways are higher; His thoughts are far above my human wisdom. No matter what the circumstance or how difficult the way looks, God's commanding word comes to me with a certain cruse of oil, ceaselessly full to capacity for my consumption and dissemination.

So Elijah arose and went.

From *All I Have Needed*
BY ELVA MINETTE MARTIN

REBUKE THE SINNER

*"Be on your guard! If your brother sins, rebuke him;
and if he repents, forgive him."*

LUKE 17:3 NASB

*B*ack in the 1950s, neighborhood accountability was a fact of life. Families took pride in raising their children properly. And on the rare occasion when someone's kid did act up, it was guaranteed that by suppertime the parents would already have heard about it through the neighborhood grapevine. Punishment was swift and commensurate with the crime.

Since my husband and I had both benefitted from the same kind of environment, we agreed completely on how we'd raise our children. However, in the early 1970s, we realized that a whole new breed of parents had evolved. They lacked the faith and fortitude to be disciplined or to discipline their own children.

Their children grew up for the most part without spiritual guidance, morality, or goals.

It still takes the knowledge of Jesus Christ to redeem our world. Here Jesus admonished His disciples to "rebuke" their brothers if they've sinned. Why? Because sin is a progressive fall. And "real love" means intervening that we might get back on track.

Have you shared your love of Jesus with a neighbor? Pray today that God might open a door or window to your witness.

From *Daily Wisdom for Women*
BY CAROL L. FITZPATRICK

TEMPTATION

Let your eyes look straight ahead,
fix your gaze directly before you.
Make level paths for your feet
and take only ways that are firm.
Do not swerve to the right or the left;
keep your foot from evil.

PROVERBS 4:25–27 NIV

*M*y husband, Bob, recently took up walking three miles every other day in order to lose some weight and shape up. I decided several weeks later to join him on his walk through town.

While we trekked down Main Street, Bob shared a valuable lesson with me. He said walking was not the hard part. The challenge was passing the pizza shop, a hot dog stand, the doughnut store, two deli shops, and an ice cream parlor.

I thought a lot about Bob's story in relation to our walks with God. It isn't our step with God that's difficult, it's our walking (or running) past the temptations along the way. We can do so only by focusing on Him.

Though temptations surround me on every side, I keep my focus on You. I know You are far greater than any traps set in my way.

The devil often tempts me in my weakest areas. When this happens, I refuse to dwell on the temptation. Instead, I give the problem to You, Lord. Whatever temptations I face, others have encountered before me. I trust You to take them all, making a way for me to escape and be victorious in You.

From *When God Sees Me Through*
BY ANITA CORRINE DONIHUE

OVERCOMING YOUR DOUBTS

Trust in the LORD with all thine heart;
and lean not unto thine own understanding.

PROVERBS 3:5 KJV

Do not give heed to your doubts for a moment. Turn from them with horror, as you would from blasphemy; for they are blasphemy. You cannot hinder the suggestions of doubt from coming to you any more than you can hinder the boys in the street from swearing as you go by; and consequently you are not sinning in the one case any more than in the other. But just as you can refuse to listen to the boys or join in their oaths, so can you also refuse to listen to the doubts or join in with them. They are not your doubts until you consent to them and adopt them as true.

Put your will in this matter over on the Lord's side, and trust Him to keep you from falling. Tell Him all about your utter weakness and your long-encouraged habits of doubt, and how helpless you are before it, and commit the whole battle to Him. Believe He is faithful, not because you feel it, or see it, but because He says He is. . . . Cultivate a continuous habit of believing, and never let your faith waver for any [reason], however plausible it may be. . . . Sooner or later you will come to know that it is true, and all doubts will vanish in the blaze of the glory of the absolute faithfulness of God!

HANNAH WHITALL SMITH
From *A Gentle Spirit*
COMPILED BY ASHLEIGH BRYCE CLAYTON

JESUS, THE GOOD SHEPHERD

"He who enters by the door is a shepherd of the sheep.
To him the doorkeeper opens,
and the sheep hear his voice,
and he calls his own sheep by name and leads them out."

JOHN 10:2–3 NASB

Sheep just aren't very bright. They need constant overseeing, tender treatment, and strict boundaries. The shepherd took them to the best pastures, found safe lodging for them during the night, and then led them out again in the morning. He was the ultimate caregiver!

In fact, the shepherd would stretch his own body out across the opening to the sheep pen. What a graphic picture of protection this provides as we consider that Christ considers Himself our Shepherd.

As the world screams out for us to follow every wind of doctrine, Christ's voice calls us back to obedience: " 'When he puts forth all his own, he goes ahead of them, and the sheep follow him because they know his voice' " (John 10:4 NASB). His voice will never call us to rebellion, sinful pleasures, or departure from His Word.

God calls us by name, just as the shepherd has pet names for his sheep. Someday, when the King of Kings, our Good Shepherd, calls us home to heaven, we'll hear the name He calls us.

From *Daily Wisdom for Women*
BY CAROL L. FITZPATRICK

THOSE BORN OF GOD OBEY HIM

Whoever believes that Jesus is the Christ is born of God,
and whoever loves the Father loves the child born of Him.
By this we know that we love the children of God,
when we love God and observe His commandments.

1 JOHN 5:1–2 NASB

When our children disobey, we feel not only extreme disappointment but a sense that they don't love us. For if they did, they would understand that our instructions are meant to guide them over the rough terrain of life. This is exactly how God feels when we fail to follow Him. For He equates love with obedience.

" 'If you love Me, you will keep My commandments' " (John 14:15 NASB). How on earth can we accomplish this task? By the power of God's Spirit within us! " 'I will ask the Father, and He will give you another Helper, that He may be with you forever; that is the Spirit of truth' " (John 14:16–17 NASB).

How can we know for sure that the Spirit of God indwells us? "And the testimony is this, that God has given us eternal life, and this life is in His Son. He who has the Son has the life; he who does not have the Son of God does not have the life" (1 John 5:11–12 NASB).

From *Daily Wisdom for Women*
BY CAROL L. FITZPATRICK

SURRENDERING THE CONTROL

*Be still before the L*ORD *and wait patiently for him.*

PSALM 37:7 NIV

I used to think that I had surrendered to God now and then. . . but I would just enjoy His company during some temporary unpleasantness and then go back to doing everything my way. When God started to change my perspective and teach me how to wait purposefully, He had His work cut out for Him. He gave me example after example of His unlimited power and wisdom and invited me to follow. I would retain what I'd learned for about, oh, two days, and then I would go back to controlling everything myself.

It was a long battle that the Lord waged with my will. I would convince myself that one day God would surely decide it was easier to come around to my way of thinking, that He would adjust His timing to meet mine. I would pray to Him only to show Him the logic of doing things on my schedule, and then I'd sit and wait quite impatiently for it to happen. . . .

Listening is hard when we wait, especially if we're listening for the wrong things. . . . We're often hopelessly annoyed by the time we spend waiting because events are often completely out of our control. The frustration that inevitably follows causes us to seek even more control, and when we can't have it, we get even more frustrated. The result is wasted time, wasted energy, and another trip to the waiting room. Here we go again, fighting instead of surrendering, trusting ourselves more than God.

From *You're Late Again, Lord!*
BY KARON PHILLIPS GOODMAN

HE TALKS TO ME

My soul longs for You like a thirsty land.

PSALM 143:6 NKJV

I felt empty and alone. . . . I felt powerless; I couldn't do anything to change my life, and God wouldn't do anything to change it.

I wonder how many times He was amused at my ranting, my fruitless, egotistical ravings for action now! Still, there He was, when I asked—again—explaining my work to me, again trying to help me see what was so plainly there.

I wanted answers, no strings attached. I was willing to listen as long as God would say what I wanted to hear. My preoccupation with the wait in my life overshadowed my own needs and weaknesses that I couldn't see. I believe that God thought it was time I finally addressed them because He knew how they were destroying me from within. My frustration with the waiting time was only the outward sign. He provided the opportunity to grow closer to Him within the wait that I detested so.

If the Lord thought that I was finally ready to listen and learn, He was right. If necessity is the mother of invention, then desperation is surely the mother of decision. I made my choice that day. I was ready to learn those lessons He had for me, to learn the art of waiting purposefully, of working on His timeline. I had no idea how long the lessons would take. The fact is that they continue today, and I accept that.

From *You're Late Again, Lord!*
BY KARON PHILLIPS GOODMAN

HE HAS A PLAN

Does he who implanted the ear not hear?
Does he who formed the eye not see?
Does he who disciplines nations not punish?
Does he who teaches man lack knowledge?
The LORD knows the thoughts of man;
he knows that they are futile.

PSALM 94:9–11 NIV

*W*aiting is inevitable for us all. We can either spend the time with complaints and arguments and disgust or use the time for worship and growth and understanding. The plan He devised long ago gives us a goal and the tools to reach it. "Those who wait on the LORD shall renew their strength. . ." (Isaiah 40:31 NKJV). Nothing zaps your strength and energy and feeling of purpose like having to wait. But we can renew our strength when we wait on the Lord.

In many interpretations of God's message, the words "wait" and "hope" are used interchangeably. That makes sense. Waiting is always filled with hope. Hope implies something yet to come. And both reveal complete dependence on the Lord. "Wait and hope in me," He says, "and while you're there, do these things. . . ."

He doesn't say wait and hope and sit quietly. He says to mount up, to run, and to walk—these are words that indicate anything but inaction. These words require work. These words come with a purpose. You can fulfill the Lord's purpose for you while you wait and hope. What a plan. I told you He was smart.

From *You're Late Again, Lord!*
BY KARON PHILLIPS GOODMAN

LOOKING INSIDE

Casting all your care upon Him, for He cares for you.

1 PETER 5:7 NKJV

*T*hose of you who tend to be a little impatient now and then probably also tend to be a little on the controlling side. That's fine if you're potty training a Great Dane, but you can't wait purposefully and control the rest of the world at the same time. Believe me, I've tried. In His unfathomable patience, God has waited on me through each pointless, misguided effort.

Ever since I was a little girl, I thought that if I could just stay a step ahead of everyone else, there would be no unpleasant surprises. I would plan ahead for every event, anticipate problems, seek remedies, devise contingency plans, and pretty much organize my world around my schedule. There's nothing wrong with a little forethought, but I made a SWAT team look slow to react. In all my struggle for control, I failed to see what I could gain by giving up that control to God.

The Lord let me go on like this for many years, through high school, college, and well into my thirties. When you look to yourself for all the answers and explanations and guidelines, it will make you doubt everything—ultimately including yourself—because you will fail miserably. When you're trying to hold on to the control that you *think* you have, you never see what God is trying to help you rediscover.

From *You're Late Again, Lord!*
BY KARON PHILLIPS GOODMAN

PATIENCE IS HIGHLY OVERRATED

But those who wait on the LORD
Shall renew their strength;
They shall mount up with wings like eagles,
They shall run and not be weary,
They shall walk and not faint.

ISAIAH 40:31 NKJV

*M*y Bible doesn't say, "Those who wait on the Lord are patient," or "Those who wait on the Lord don't do anything else." It says, "Those who wait on the LORD shall renew their strength. . ." (Isaiah 40:31 NKJV). Waiting and hoping in the Lord can do nothing else *but* renew my strength.

Even in my shattered, impatient state, God can teach me and use me. Working while I wait means believing in God's ability to handle all things in His time and using the time He's given me for a purpose. I can yearn for patience, or I can wait with a purpose. . . .

Understanding what God wants for me and how to get there is a long haul. Sometimes we go over the same issues again and again, as I search to rediscover His guidance or tap into His courage. I get angry and frustrated. I forget my lessons. But God doesn't forget His plan. He won't give up on me. . . .

God is the original multitasker. He tends to you and me at the same time. When we fret about the lack of answers and actions that we need, we waste the chance to grow. " 'Be still, and know that I am God,' " He says (Psalm 46:10 NIV). "Knowing" God means learning about God, drawing nearer to God, developing an unmovable trust and faith in God. That's *purpose.* That's God at work while you wait.

From *You're Late Again, Lord!*
BY KARON PHILLIPS GOODMAN

SIMPLE FAITH

Let us draw near to God with a sincere heart
in full assurance of faith. . . .
Let us hold unswervingly to the hope we profess,
for he who promised is faithful.

HEBREWS 10:22–23 NIV

*I*t's extremely difficult for us to live in faith, because doing so means giving up on our own efforts, and we are a nation of doers. If asked, most of us would say we have faith, that we believe God cares for us and will always give us His best. But we worry about the details a lot. God will provide for us, but will we like the way it all works out? Can we help? Can our science and technology change the timetable a little? How much meddling can we engage in and still say we have faith?

I don't personally think God expects us to sit back and wait for Him. He gives us knowledge for a reason, so why not make good use of it? If we goof up, do we really not believe God is capable of correcting our errors and showing us a better way?

And yet we know there is much that requires faith, so much we cannot do ourselves. Here is where we meet simple faith. We do the best we can as earthly creatures; the rest we must leave to God in faith. Sometimes faith is dynamic and purposeful; other times it is simply waiting and trusting.

From *Everyday Abundance*
BY TONI SORTOR

WHAT IF I FAIL?

Let him have all your worries and cares,
for he is always thinking about you
and watching everything that concerns you.

1 PETER 5:7 TLB

I have chosen the problem of perfectionism because all of us have a little of the perfectionist in us. Having been made in the image of God, we can conceive what perfection is, and we long for it. However, because of our sinful nature and selfish ways, we fail to attain it. . . .

If our self-esteem is not rooted in Christ, we feel that the only way we can prove our own worth is by being perfect. But if our sense of self-esteem depends on our being perfect, then we will always fall short. No matter how good we do, we will be frustrated and discouraged, because the truth is, none of us can be perfect at every aspect of our lives. We will sometimes let our husbands down; some days we will be impatient and selfish with our children; our houses will not always be clean and sparkling; and sooner or later, no matter how good we are at our jobs, we will make some obvious mistake that we can't excuse away. When these things happen, we are faced with the glaring truth: None of us is perfect. Only God is, and we are all only human. But this need for perfection is the very reason many women struggle with a low concept of themselves.

From *Created for a Purpose*
BY DARLENE SALA

CHRIST'S PEACE

Let the peace of Christ rule in your hearts.

COLOSSIANS 3:15 NIV

*C*hrist's peace is not a passive absence of conflict but an active arbitrator in the middle of conflict. When circumstances in my life are in an uproar, I am to let Christ's peace rule or control me.

Some of life's most discouraging battles are not the big dramatic ones, but the little everyday stresses we all face. . .like when your to-do list is longer than the piece of paper you're writing it on, and you're coming down with the flu. On days like that, when you simply don't have the strength to face the daily battle of your busy schedule, how on earth do you "let Christ's peace rule"?

It seems impossible. But that's precisely when we need to let Christ's peace rule. At that point we say, "God, this situation is entirely out of my control. There's nothing I can do to bring order out of this chaos. Everything is a mess. Now, You take charge. I'm going to live this day one moment at a time, endeavoring to do what You want me to do. But I'm putting You in charge, not me." It's amazing the peace that can flood your heart—God's peace— as you turn over the responsibility to Him.

Christ's peace is not a denial of the circumstances but instead a commitment to the fact that He is enough for your circumstances. When we put Him in charge of our lives, the battle is already won!

From *Encouraging Words for Women*
BY DARLENE SALA

GOD AND MY TO-DO LIST

*Take your everyday, ordinary life—
your sleeping, eating, going-to-work,
and walking-around life—
and place it before God as an offering.*

ROMANS 12:1 THE MESSAGE

*M*any of us feel God is disappointed if we don't accomplish all we hope. We feel guilty when at the end of some days not even one item on the list is crossed off.

But Jesus did not come to earth to help us get more done. He came to make it possible for us to have a personal relationship with God. Not just "fire insurance" to keep us out of hell, but day-by-day walking and talking together.

I like that phrase "the fellowship of the Holy Spirit" used in 2 Corinthians 13:14. God the Holy Spirit lives within us, and that means we can have fellowship with Him through His Spirit. That means we can sense His presence right where we are in the middle of our circumstances.

It's not enough to organize your life so that you get the most important things done first—unless the very first thing on your list is your relationship with God. It's not enough to learn to win friends and influence people—unless the #1 Friend in your life is Jesus.

God wants a relationship with you where every part of your life is open to Him; He wants your first concern to be how you can fellowship with Him on a closer, warmer, and more personal level. When you have that sort of relationship, you can trust your to-do list to Him. He knows better than you what you really need to accomplish.

From *Encouraging Words for Women*
BY DARLENE SALA

I DON'T LIKE MY JOB

God has said,
"Never will I leave you;
never will I forsake you."
So we say with confidence,
"The Lord is my helper; I will not be afraid."

HEBREWS 13:5–6 NIV

*D*ear Father, I pray You will help me with my job. Things aren't going right. I dread going to work, and I need Your direction. On days I feel I'm doing more than my share, may my attitudes be right. Give me wisdom, I pray. When I do menial tasks, help me remember when Your Son, though King of Kings, came down from heaven and often acted as a servant. Let me not be too proud to serve.

Help me to be honest in estimating my own abilities, to not put myself down or become a braggart. Teach me to appreciate a job well done, to feel an inner sense of accomplishment. I lean on You, not only on my skills. I know I can earn my pay and make a living; or I can give of myself and make a life.

Go before me when there is friction and backbiting. Let my motives be pure and uplifting, depending on Your help, so Your light can shine through.

"Whatever you do, work at it with all your heart, as working for the Lord, not for men, since you know that you will receive an inheritance from the Lord as a reward. It is the Lord Christ you are serving" (Colossians 3:23–24 NIV).

From *When I'm on My Knees*
BY ANITA CORRINE DONIHUE

MOMENTS OF BEAUTY

To the only God our Savior be glory,
majesty, power and authority,
through Jesus Christ our Lord,
before all ages, now and forevermore!
Amen.

JUDE 1:25 NIV

When I see breathtaking beauty or sense a poignant moment—whether it's the birth of a baby, a dazzling sunset, or a dramatic mountain peak towering above me—I have ambivalent feelings. I feel awe, wonder, and joy—and at the same time I feel pain. I think it's because I know I cannot hold on to the beauty and significance I'm seeing. I want to reach out my hands and capture it and hold tight forever—but I know I can't.

I believe that in heaven we will no longer have ambivalent feelings because the beauty there will never fade. Heaven will be perfect—and so will we. We'll have all eternity to appreciate what we're experiencing.

We can comprehend perfection now. But, living in a sinful world, we cannot achieve it or hold on to it. But we have a Savior who is perfect. That's why we find such rest and joy and peace in Him, for He is all that we long for in beauty and significance. And not only can we hold on to Him, which we can't do with the beauty on earth, but better yet, He holds on to us! Jude says that God "is able to keep you from falling and to present you before his glorious presence without fault and with great joy" (Jude 1:24 NIV).

From *Encouraging Words for Women*
BY DARLENE SALA

NEW ETERNAL HOME

*"I am the way and the truth and the life.
No one comes to the Father except through me."*

JOHN 14:6 NIV

*Wh*enever I think of heaven, a deep, homesick feeling stirs within me. I feel I have been there before my time on this earth began. There is an overpowering love drawing me to run and fall into my heavenly Father's arms.

What will heaven be like? The Bible says there will be no more sin or violence, sickness or pain, no tears or grief. We often grow weary of fending off these things that cause anguish and stress. We long for a carefree, eternal life with God in heaven. What a delight it will be when we get to see our Christian loved ones and friends who have gone home before us!

But there is more to heaven than this. The glorious, awesome Triune of God the Father, God the Son, and God the Holy Spirit is there. Heaven will be more than a blessed revival or camp meeting. We will actually get to meet Him face-to-face!

As I fall before Him in reverence, I can imagine Jesus, my Savior, stepping forward, bending down, and taking my hand. As He helps me to my feet, I may hear Him say, "It's all right, My child. I paid the price for your sins. Welcome home."

From *When God Sees Me Through*
BY ANITA CORRINE DONIHUE

SHHH!

And, behold, the word of the LORD came to him,
and he said unto him,
What doest thou here, Elijah?

1 KINGS 19:9 KJV

*H*ear the quiet! Absolute stillness captures attention more rapidly than any word, sound, or signal. Our world is so busy and ever so noisy. *Shhh!* God's voice is not usually heard in the rumble of traffic or in the confusion of rush, but in the quietness of a seeking heart.

To hear God's voice, I must be expecting Him to speak to me at any moment. I must be tuned to the correct channel, that is, turned away from sin and self. If I let myself get caught up in the world around me, my inner ear may not be attentive to His voice. God ministered to His servant Elijah when he was weary. He allowed sleep, gave food, and more sleep. This went on for a period of time not specified in Scripture, but it was sufficient time for Elijah's refreshment. The Word says he went in the strength of that refreshment for forty days.

I find it encouraging to see how God has numbered the days of testing. I need to take time to notice how He has provided refreshment during stressful times. I recognize that God's provision has always been enough to meet my spiritual, physical, and emotional needs of the moment! I can look up: God is! *Shhh!* I will listen! God speaks to an attentive heart.

From *All I Have Needed*
BY ELVA MINETTE MARTIN

C. J. AND THE CAT

"Ask and it will be given to you."

MATTHEW 7:7 NIV

Ten-year-old C. J. had been in my Sunday school class for two years. I knew him well. One Sunday morning he shared a prayer request with us. He wanted prayer for his sick cat. I lightheartedly added the request to several others as we prayed.

The next Sunday C. J. told how his cat was getting worse and the veterinarian was concerned about the cat's recovery. It came time for morning worship service. When my husband, Bob, asked for prayer requests, C. J. raised his hand and asked for prayer for his cat.

Bob looked surprised. Some people smiled. Others stifled chuckles. Bob gingerly added C. J.'s request to several others, asking that God would be with C. J.

After church, C. J. came to me. "I want us to pray for my cat, not me," he announced.

At that moment, God spoke to my heart. The two of us sat on the back pew in the sanctuary and prayed earnestly for God to heal C. J.'s cat. Then I turned to my dear student and told him to tell everyone he had prayed for his cat and to give God the praise.

What am I saying? I wondered. *Lord, this is really putting our prayers to the test.*

The next week in Sunday school class C. J. said the cat was recovering. Our class thanked God together.

Later that day, I praised God again for the unexpected little blessing of C. J. and his cat.

From *When I'm Praising God*
BY ANITA CORRINE DONIHUE

THE VET'S

*Do not despise the LORD'S discipline
and do not resent his rebuke,
because the LORD disciplines those he loves.*

PROVERBS 3:11–12 NIV

*O*ne of the cats has to go to the vet's today. She just had her checkup; then we went back to get flea medicine, and now her ears are itching. I wouldn't mind all this so much if it didn't involve getting her into and out of the cat carrier. Doing so requires tactics only found in the Special Forces: infiltration, encirclement, and neutralization. Then there's the effort required to fold four rigid, outspread legs down into the carrier at one time without losing your grip on the cat's body or being seriously scratched.

Cats are not stupid. They must know this is all for their benefit, that they will no longer itch or hurt when it's over and we bring them home. But still they fight it. They act as if we are trying to kill them when we are actually saving them.

Of course, I'm no better when God decides I am in need of correction or remedy. I fight it every time He tries to get a hold on me and put me where I need to be. I don't want to go—the carrier is small and frightening—so I make corralling me as difficult as possible. Fortunately, God is far more patient than we are with the cats. As with the cats when it's time to go home, all He does is leave the door open, and I walk right in.

From *Everyday Abundance*
BY TONI SORTOR

PETS

For everything God created is good,
and nothing is to be rejected if it is
received with thanksgiving.

1 TIMOTHY 4:4 NIV

*O*ur house always resembled a zoo when our children were young. We had dogs and cats and short-lived fish. When everyone grew up, I declared, "No more pets. If you want them, get your own." When the last cat died, I relished the peace and quiet. There was no more fur on my black slacks, no more pet food scattered around the kitchen. I didn't have to break up cat fights at three in the morning. It was so peaceful and quiet that two days later I adopted a kitten. A year later, a tomcat adopted us. So much for no more pets.

I have held out against dogs, however. You don't have to walk a cat, and they do fine if you leave them food and go away for a weekend. Any yearning for a dog is satisfied by borrowing our daughter's dog—our "granddog"—who loves us to distraction and reminds me why I don't want a dog around full time.

I'm thankful for the pets we have had. They taught our children responsibility. They taught them how to love and be loved. They taught them how to grieve the loss of a loved one. But when the cats die, that's it. No more pets. Or so I say now.

From *Everyday Abundance*
BY TONI SORTOR

DOORS

I waited patiently for the LORD;
he turned to me and heard my cry.

PSALM 40:1 NIV

*W*hat is it with cats and doors? My cats allow no interior door to be shut, just in case a cat napping in the kitchen sun has an urgent need to go nap on a bed. Our cats also hold me personally responsible for the weather, which causes more door problems. Max, the indoor-outdoor cat, will charge out the front door with enthusiasm, suddenly realize he's getting wet, and yowl to come back in. Within two minutes he will ask to go out the back door, and heaven help me if it's raining in the backyard, too! Tillie, the indoor cat who is happiest when Max is outside, wonders why I just don't make the sun shine and be done with her brother.

I admit there are times when I act like my cats. I don't like it when a door I want open in my life is suddenly slammed shut. It makes me angry and frustrated, and sometimes, like Max, I run to another door to discover I don't like what's on the other side of that one, either. I sulk and torment anyone in the house until someone fixes the problem—which no one can do. Sometimes it's raining outside all the doors, and I need to practice patience and trust.

From *Everyday Abundance*
BY TONI SORTOR

BUOYANCY IS A WONDERFUL ASSET

*Does not the potter have the right to make out of
the same lump of clay some pottery for noble purposes
and some for common use?*

ROMANS 9:21 NIV

*E*ven in my slim-and-trim days, I stored enough body fat to bob like a cork whenever I touched water. . . .

My buoyancy provided more laughter than a slapstick comedy as we routinely beelined for the hotel pool to devise water games. I boasted one award-winning game: Who could tread water the longest? "Hey, that's no fair!" Jimmy protested at the mere mention of the game as his brother Jeff chimed in. "Yeah, we all know Mom is unsinkable!"

After the jesting subsided, my husband soothed me with his trademark brand of consolation. "Look on the positive side, honey," he said, concealing a grin. "Your built-in life preserver might come in handy someday. Think of how many people you could have saved on the *Titanic*."

I leveled a stern scowl in his direction. "Yeah, that's right, just throw my body overboard and instruct people to latch on!"

Perhaps my heartless husband had a point, though. God views us much differently than we view ourselves; rather than dwelling on the negatives, the Lord maximizes our lives to their fullest potential.

With that in mind, I choose to consider my buoyancy as a positive trait. After all, let's not underestimate my unique life-saving capabilities!

From *Laughter Therapy*
BY TINA KRAUSE

EVER-LIVING LAUGHTER

A merry heart does good, like medicine,
But a broken spirit dries the bones.

PROVERBS 17:22 NKJV

There are many things we can do to improve our health: proper food and rest, plenty of exercise, regular checkups from our doctors, etc. One more essential thing I find is the medicine of laughter—a deep-down dose of ever-living laughter from the belly.

Did you know a few minutes of deep belly laughing is as good as time on a rowing machine? It burns calories, eases tension, calms emotions, and helps relationships.

On the day Bob and I were married, my future father-in-law drove me to the church to check on the catering equipment. He gave me some advice that has stayed with me for forty-two years.

"Always keep your sense of humor, Neat," he quipped. "It will carry you and your love for one another a long way.

"When I get in trouble with Ma," he said, "I stick my head in the door and ask if I can throw my hat in first. Ma and I both always burst out in laughter."

We live in a complex world. Things don't always go well. Life may not continually be happy for us, but it can still be filled with God's joy. Let's not dwell on the sadness and the negative but think on good things.

From *When God Calls Me Blessed*
BY ANITA CORRINE DONIHUE

A WILLING HEART

"O Jerusalem, Jerusalem,
you who kill the prophets and stone those sent to you,
how often I have longed to gather your children together,
as a hen gathers her chicks under her wings,
but you were not willing!"

LUKE 13:34 NIV

I hate to bore you by rattling on about diets, so please "indulge" me for a few moments. I struggled for several months, attempting to obtain "abstinence." Yet it remained as illusive as grasping a cloud. My problem? I wasn't willing to let God take control.

Finally, as I obediently worked the first three steps of the Overeaters Anonymous program, peace followed. I admitted to being powerless because the compulsion to eat had made my life unmanageable. And I came to believe that God's power could restore me to sane eating. Then I made a decision to turn my will and life over to the Lord's care. And the "gift" of dietary abstinence became a part of my life.

This was actually the first time I realized that God was truly almighty. When He made it easy for me to walk through life without being controlled by food, I knew He was real.

How like the Israelites I am! God showed them the path they were to walk in. He even defined the boundaries for them. And yet time after time they leaped beyond the lines of safety and tried to live without Him.

Is it time for you to let God steer the course?

From *Daily Wisdom for Women*
BY CAROL L. FITZPATRICK

EXERCISE

Be merciful to me, LORD, for I am faint;
O LORD, heal me, for my bones are in agony.

PSALM 6:2 NIV

We have a treadmill in the living room to remind us to exercise. I break into a sweat every time I dust the thing. Once or twice a week I actually turn it on and do some leisurely walking, but I get bored after ten minutes and go find something better to do, even though I know I need twenty minutes of trudging to do myself any good.

Fishing involves lots of walking and climbing and stumbling around in the woods, but we only do that about six months of the year, and a lot of times we fish from a canoe, which doesn't give us much exercise unless we flip it over and have to swim.

I'm afraid that my exercise is mostly haphazard and accidental. I have to weed the flowerbeds once a week, or chaos reigns out there. It's a long walk to the mailbox (give me credit for not driving the 270 feet!). When my daughter's dog is visiting, I have to walk her *or else.* You get the idea. Somehow, this type of exercise seems to work. I'm not losing weight, but I'm strong and healthy in spite of myself. I figure if the Lord wanted me to run, He'd send a mean dog to run from or an energetic two year old to keep up with.

From *Everyday Abundance*
BY TONI SORTOR

HEALTH

" 'But I will restore you to health
and heal your wounds,'
declares the LORD. "

JEREMIAH 30:17 NIV

I just had my annual mammogram (any women over the age of forty may feel free to groan). While it's still not something to look forward to, they've made mechanical improvements, and the whole thing is much easier. Two months ago I had my annual flu shot, so now I'm healthy while everyone else is coughing. My eye doctor assures me that my failing eyesight is just old age, and my internist says those little irregular heartbeats are perfectly harmless although annoying.

On the other hand, one of my grandmothers died in the flu epidemic of 1918. The other died equally young from a heart attack, while my great-grandmother went blind in middle age. Longevity does not run in my family, yet I am still as healthy as a horse, thanks to my collection of doctors. Every time I have to change insurance plans and find a whole new set of doctors, I try to be thankful that I have insurance at all and the health system is doing far better for me than it did for my ancestors.

Good health is a great blessing, even if maintaining it is often a pain in the neck. Yes, the health system is still full of inequities and in need of improvement, but the older I get, the more I appreciate it, especially since my ancestors rarely survived long enough to qualify for Medicare.

From *Everyday Abundance*
BY TONI SORTOR

GROWING OLDER

"Therefore I tell you, do not worry about your life,
what you will eat or drink;
or about your body, what you will wear."

MATTHEW 6:25 NIV

*L*ord, my friends tease me about being over the hill. They say the best of life is gone. When I hear this, I laugh.

I wonder what You have in store for me this next year? I have no fear of growing older. Life is out there to enjoy. Thank You for giving me one more year to do so.

I will not be poured into an ancient mold. I may be growing older, but I refuse to act old. Old age is an attitude. I'm determined to live life abundantly through Your joy and strength.

I'm not ashamed of pain-filled fingers gnarled from arthritis. They show the work I have done for others. I see the wrinkles collecting on my face. Character lines, I call them. I especially like the ones put there from years of smiles. No matter my health, I can always find ways to serve You, such as letters to the lonely. Best of all, I can hold others up in faithful prayer.

I thank You, Lord, for life and that You offer it to me in an abundance of spirit and joy. Even when I reach my sunset years, I lift my praise to You. May I reflect Your Holy Spirit all the days of my life.

From *When I'm on My Knees*
BY ANITA CORRINE DONIHUE

PRAISE THE LORD FOR HEAVEN

"He will wipe every tear from their eyes.
There will be no more death or
mourning or crying or pain,
for the old order of things has passed away."

REVELATION 21:4 NIV

My thoughts often turn toward heaven, Lord. When earthly trials and worries surround me, I long to be with You. I feel homesick, as though I have some subconscious memory of having been in heaven before. Could I have been with You there before I was placed in my mother's womb? Someday I'll have the answers.

I don't feel a part of the evil in this world, and I'm certainly not attracted to what it has to offer. All the money I could earn, the treasure I can obtain, the land I may plan to buy are nothing in light of my eternal home with You. Earthly things lose their value. They wear out, rust, fade, and are sometimes stolen. The eternal treasures I store in heaven with You can never be taken from me. So I'll invest my meager riches in You and Your work.

Although my body will die, my soul grows closer to You with each passing day. All the trials and sufferings are minor and won't last. Thank You for the heavenly home I'll go to someday. There will be no sickness there, no pain, no tears. Only eternal life filled with joy and gladness awaits me. There I can be with You and praise You forever.

From *When I'm on My Knees*
BY ANITA CORRINE DONIHUE

MY SACRIFICE OF PRAISE

Praise ye the LORD.
Praise God in his sanctuary:
praise him in the firmament of his power.

PSALM 150:1 KJV

To You, Father, I offer my sacrifice—an offering of praise. I honor You, Father. I thank You and sing praises to You above all else. Each morning I rise with praises on my lips, thanking You for Your loving-kindness. Each evening I thank You for being with me through the day.

I give You everything in my life—the good in me, the faults—so You can help me change. Let me be a living praise to You, dear Lord. May my attitude and motives laud and honor You. May my life be the kind that is acceptable in Your sight.

You sacrificed Your Son. He suffered and died outside Jerusalem where His blood spilled and washed my sins away. Because of this, I will continually offer my sacrifice of praise to You, dear Lord. I will tell everyone who listens about Your glory and love. I will give thanks for all things to You, God the Father, in the name of Your Son, Jesus Christ.

You are worthy of all praise. Worthy to receive power, glory, honor, and adoration beyond limit.

Praise be to You, O God!

From *When I'm Praising God*
BY ANITA CORRINE DONIHUE

PRAISE AND DANCE

Praise the LORD! Praise God in His sanctuary;
Praise Him in His mighty expanse.
Praise Him for His mighty deeds;
Praise Him according to His excellent greatness.

PSALM 150:1–2 NASB

*I*n other words, "Praise Him with all you've got to make noise with!" Isn't that what true worship is, using our entire beings to give Him the glory He deserves?

I know people who believe that dancing is a sin. But God said He wanted His people dancing and praising Him. This worshipful motion accompanied the psalms as they were sung.

In just this one psalm we are given a formula for worship.

Whom are we to praise? The Lord! Where are we to praise? Wherever His congregation gathers. For what are we praising? For who He is, what He's done, and the way He's done it. How are we to praise? With our voices, our instruments, and our bodies as we dance in worship.

You've heard people say, "I don't need church, I can worship God anywhere." They usually mean that a formal church service usurps precious moments spent in personal pursuits. They are denying any accountability to God.

The church is God's provision for all the spiritual and physical needs of His people. In a society that has become so mobile as to practically abandon the idea of closeness with extended family, the church picks up the slack.

From *Daily Wisdom for Women*
BY CAROL L. FITZPATRICK

SACRIFICE OF PRAISE

How can I repay the LORD
for all his goodness to me?
I will lift up the cup of salvation
and call on the name of the LORD.
I will fulfill my vows to the LORD
in the presence of all his people.

PSALM 116:12–14 NIV

*F*ather, I offer You my sacrifice of praise. Forever will I honor Your name. I lift my voice in song, giving You praise. In the morning I praise You for a new day. At evening, I rejoice in all You have done.

As long as I have breath, I will praise You. I give You my whole being, that it may be pleasing unto You and acceptable in Your sight. This is the least I can do for You, dear Lord.

I want to constantly praise You to my friends and loved ones so they, too, can know all You have done for me. I long for them to learn to know and love You and experience real joy.

No other is so worthy of my praise. You are power, wisdom, honor, glory, might, and blessing. Your words fill my life. Your lessons teach me wisdom. Let everything I do and say be pleasing unto You, so I may be a true reflection of You to others and glorify my Father, who is in heaven. Again, I offer the only thing I can give You, my sacrifice of praise. Praise be the Lord!

From *When I'm on My Knees*
BY ANITA CORRINE DONIHUE

THANK YOU FOR YOUR WORD, LORD

*I have hidden your word in my heart
that I might not sin against you.*

PSALM 119:11 NIV

Thank You for my Bible, Your Word. How dear it is to me. Your Word never fails me. Thank You for providing these Scriptures so I can find direction in my life.

How perceptive are Your teachings. What blessings I receive from reading its words. You are so wonderful to give me the secrets to having a joy-filled life.

Still there are mysteries to unfold as I read its fathomless insights. How can I ever fully understand all of the lessons? Will I ever be able to completely know the mind of God? You are too great for me to do so.

How could I possibly have a pure heart without Your Scriptures to remind and guide each day? I would have no direction or hope.

I seek You with all my being so I might not stray. I memorize and hide Your words in my heart. When temptation and testing come, I can draw on what I have learned as Your Son, Jesus, did when He was tempted.

Praise You, dear Lord. Teach me Your countless lessons. I will repeat them on my lips and hide them in my heart as You have shown me. I will rejoice in all I learn. I will meditate on Your Word and praise You through my nights and days.

From *When I'm on My Knees*
BY ANITA CORRINE DONIHUE

ANSWERED PRAYERS

"Because he loves me," says the LORD,
"I will rescue him;
I will protect him, for he
acknowledges my name.
He will call upon me,
and I will answer him;
I will be with him in trouble,
I will deliver him and honor him.
With long life will I satisfy him
and show him my salvation."

PSALM 91:14–16 NIV

I prayed to You, dear Lord, to bless and help me as I worked for You. I sought You out time after time during my daily tasks and asked for You to keep me from wrong and disaster. To my amazement, You answered my prayers!

Why do I feel so surprised when miracles happen? More than lack of faith, I simply marvel at Your works, wisdom, and knowledge. Thank You, Lord.

The next time I anxiously call on You, please help me remember all You have done. In the meantime, right here, right now, I praise You again for answers to my prayers.

From *When I'm Praising God*
BY ANITA CORRINE DONIHUE

LAUGHTER IS CONTAGIOUS

Our mouths were filled with laughter,
our tongues with songs of joy.

PSALM 126:2 NIV

When I visited Jamaica, I learned a lesson in laughter. At first, the people and their seemingly aggressive behavior startled me. That night, I prayed, "Lord, help me to see these people through Your eyes."

The next day, as I strolled the streets of Ocho Rios, I noticed something different. Everyone with whom I made contact smiled at me.

Puzzled yet pleased, I mentioned it to my husband. "It's no wonder," he replied with a shrug. "You've been smiling at everyone ever since we left the hotel."

God answered my prayer. He planted a warm smile on my face to share with those I had once misunderstood. And they reciprocated.

Have you ever giggled and couldn't stop? Others will soon join in because laughter is contagious.

Jesus said, " 'Give, and it will be given unto you' " (Luke 6:38 NIV). Offer a smile to individuals you meet today—the bank teller, the store clerk, the cashier, a coworker. Then share your results with a friend. This exercise may not only change you, but it might bless someone who needs to smile.

From *Laughter Therapy*
BY TINA KRAUSE

NEVER SAY NEVER

Who Himself bore our sins in His own body on the tree,
that we, having died to sins,
might live for rightousness—by
whose stripes you were healed.

1 PETER 2:24 NKJV

We often beg for some of our friends and loved ones to accept Jesus as their Savior and Lord. We pray and pray and see no change. Sometimes things become worse. The one we pray for goes deeper into sin. All the signs may point to discouragement, hopelessness, no apparent chance of turning around. We are tempted to give up, write them off, and say they will never change.

Nothing is impossible when we trust God. It may take a long time, but God works through everything. He never gives up. He loves our friends and loved ones more than we are capable of doing. Unlike us, He can talk to their hearts, and they can't escape His words. There's a spiritual battle going on for the souls of these dear ones. As we present our prayers to God, we can be assured of the One who wins over sin and destruction.

Some of our prayers may go unanswered while we are still alive. Praise be to God, our prayers lifted to Him go on, even after our lives here on earth are finished! We can look forward to the answers being revealed to us when we reach heaven.

When all is bleak and appears impossible, keep turning your troubles over to God. Never say never. Always say, "Forever, with God!"

From *When God Sees Me Through*
BY ANITA CORRINE DONIHUE

HONORING GOD

I will bless the LORD at all times:
his praise shall continually be in my mouth.

PSALM 34:1 KJV

*W*hat can we give God that He hasn't already given us? There is only one thing we can give: our praise—our wholehearted, unconditional offering of thanksgiving.

We most often call on God when things go wrong. As the situation becomes urgent, we pray all the harder. Fear and discouragement tend to take over. How can we thank Him during such hopeless and troubled times?

Praise to God breaks our chains of fear and discouragement. Try stuffing a piece of paper in your pocket and carry it with you everywhere. Focus on the goodness of God and on the many blessings He has bestowed on you in the past. Each time you think of a blessing, stop and write it down.

When you have a quiet time, pull out your notes and begin thanking God for His goodness. Then feel His wonderful, warm presence and the freedom He gives you!

Bless and praise Him at all times. Exalt His name. Tell Him again and again He is Lord and Master in your life.

When you do this with a sincere heart, God will deliver you from your fears and direct you in the ways you are to go. The more we lift Him up, the more He places His angels around us and delivers us and those we pray for from evil and harm.

Taste and see that God is good!

From *When I Hear His Call*
BY ANITA CORRINE DONIHUE

VOCALIZING A PRAYER

"And when you are praying,
do not use meaningless repetition
as the Gentiles do, for they suppose that they will be
heard for their many words."

MATTHEW 6:7 NASB

Remember kneeling beside your bed and praying when you were a kid? Why did it all seem so simple then? We just talked to God like He was really there and kept our requests short and simple.

Then, as you got older, the lengthy and spiritual prayers of the "older saints" became intimidating. So, where's the balance? Reading a little further in this passage from Matthew, at verse 9, Jesus gives us His own example for prayer. If you can remember the acrostic ACTS, you'll have an excellent formula for prayer: Adoration, Confession, Thanksgiving, and Supplication.

As we come before the Lord we first need to honor Him as Creator, Master, Savior, and Lord. Reflect on who He is and praise Him. And because we're human we need to confess and repent of our daily sins. Following this we should be in a mode of thanksgiving. Finally, our prayer requests should be upheld. My usual order for requests is self, family members, and life's pressing issues. Keeping a prayer journal allows for a written record of God's answers.

Your prayers certainly don't have to be elaborate or polished. God does not judge your way with words. He knows your heart. He wants to hear from you.

From *Daily Wisdom for Women*
BY CAROL L. FITZPATRICK

WHEN GOD SAYS "NO"

We do not know what we ought to pray for,
but the Spirit himself intercedes for us
with groans that words cannot express.
And he who searches our hearts knows the mind of the Spirit,
because the Spirit intercedes for
the saints in accordance with God's will.

ROMANS 8:26–27 NIV

We sometimes say, "I received an answer to prayer today!" Of course, we always mean that God said, "Yes," to one of our requests. But "No" is an answer to prayer, too. And thank God that as the good parent He is, God loves me enough to sometimes say, "No."

Of course I always ask God for what I want, but with my limited knowledge and foresight, I don't always know what is best for me. If I ask for something that is not for my own good, I can be assured that God will say, "No."

God the Father answered Jesus' prayer with a "No." On the night Jesus was betrayed and arrested in the Garden of Gethsemane, three times He prayed, " 'My Father, if it is possible, may this cup be taken from me' " (Matthew 26:39 NIV). God the Father answered His Son's prayer, but His answer was, "No." Because the Father said, "No," you and I have salvation from our sins and will spend eternity with Him.

God helps us in our ignorance and lack of wisdom.

When you're praying for something specific, be encouraged. Today God may say, "Yes." Then again, He may say, "Wait awhile." But if He says, "No," remember that truly our heavenly Father knows best!

From *Encouraging Words for Women*
BY DARLENE SALA

ORDER IN OUR PRAYERS

First of all, then, I urge that entreaties and prayers,
petitions and thanksgivings, be made on behalf of all men,
for kings and all who are in authority,
so that we may lead a tranquil
and quiet life in all godliness and dignity.
This is good and acceptable in the sight of God our Savior,
who desires all men to be saved
and to come to the knowledge of the truth.

1 TIMOTHY 2:1–4 NASB

The demands of this world, and the pace at which our technology is racing, can sometimes overwhelm us, causing feelings of panic, powerlessness, and even paranoia. Is there a solution that brings life back into perspective? Yes. And God calls it prayer.

Our human sense of ineptness—we simply aren't equal to the task of being in charge of the universe—causes us to react to pressure. So, we've got to release the hand controls back to God. And when we practice this on an individual level, the prayers we offer within our congregations become more effective.

Prayer isn't some mystical entity to be attained by a few saintly little ladies in the church. Instead, it is an act of worship on the part of the created toward the Creator. Prayer is simply "talking to God" about everything that affects our lives.

From *Daily Wisdom for Women*
BY CAROL L. FITZPATRICK

IS TEMPTATION SIN?

Blessed is the man that endureth temptation:
for when he is tried, he shall receive the crown of life,
which the Lord hath promised to them that love him.

JAMES 1:12 KJV

Temptation cannot be sin; and the truth is, it is no more a sin to hear these whispers and suggestions of evil in our souls than it is for us to hear the wicked talk of bad men as we pass along the street. The sin comes, in either case, only by our stopping and joining in with them. If, when the wicked suggestions come, we turn from them at once, as we would from wicked talk, and pay no more attention to them than we would to the talk, we do not sin. But, if we carry them on our minds, and roll them under our tongues, and dwell on them with a half consent of our will to them as true, then we sin. We may be enticed by temptations a thousand times a day without sin, and we cannot help these enticings and are not to blame for them. But if we begin to think that these enticings are actual sin on our part, then the battle is half lost already, and the sin can hardly fail to gain a complete victory.

HANNAH WHITALL SMITH
From *A Gentle Spirit*
COMPILED BY ASHLEIGH BRYCE CLAYTON

FROOT LOOPS IN THE TOILET

I can do everything through
him who gives me strength.

PHILIPPIANS 4:13 NIV

*T*hose who think they must enlist in the navy to have an adventure obviously haven't tried living with preschoolers.

The day began innocently enough. I pulled Mary down from standing on the windowsills a couple of times—no big deal. I'm beginning to think she's part feline. The girls were playing rather nicely together in Mary's room with only an occasional "Stop it! I'm gonna tell Mama!"

Then, out of nowhere, I heard an awful death cry, a piercing scream, and then another cry that sent chills up my back. As I raced in slow motion the three miles down the hall, I just knew I would round the corner and face blood and broken bones everywhere. As I entered the room, an alarming but somewhat comical sight greeted me.

Mary had crawled on top of her little play kitchenette and decided to do a little walking around. When she stepped from the refrigerator to the stove, however, she forgot about the little sink, and down she went—waist deep in a toy kitchen.

To say she was hysterical would be an understatement. I worked frantically for twenty minutes trying to push and/or pull her out, all to no avail. I finally called the church and left word for Roy to come home and free his daughter from the kitchen sink.

Later that evening, I found Froot Loops in the toilet. I was too tired to care.

From *Time Out*
BY LEIGH ANN THOMAS

GROWING UP, LETTING GO

*"Build up, build up,
prepare the road!
Remove the obstacles
out of the way of my people."*

ISAIAH 57:14 NIV

"I can do it by myself!"

"I know you can, honey, but Mommy just wants to help you."

"I don't need your help!"

I've dreamed of this moment for years—the time when the girls would actually start doing more for themselves. But now something just does not feel quite right.

This vague feeling of loss is a continuous process. From their infancy until the present, our children's level of dependency on Roy and me has changed dramatically.

As parents, we knew this would happen. In fact, we prayed that our children would grow up to be strong, independent adults. But it still isn't easy to let go.

I'll never forget Laura's first day of school. My legs were like lead as I left her in a classroom of near strangers. My vision was cloudy with tears, and I knew I had to get out of there fast before everyone saw Laura's mommy cry like a baby.

Of course when Mary starts "big school," I'll experience it all over again, but that's all right. All these little "letting go's" are preparing me for the big ones later on. And I know that when the day arrives and the girls walk away into college, marriage, or a career, I'll feel pretty much the same way. And I'll breathe pretty much the same prayer, "Oh God, how I love these girls. . .please take care of them for us!"

From *Time Out*
BY LEIGH ANN THOMAS

OUR PRAYER REQUESTS

*In the morning, O Lord, you hear my voice;
in the morning I lay my requests before you
and wait in expectation.*

PSALM 5:3 NIV

When my children were young the only way I could ensure having a special quiet time of prayer was to get up earlier than anyone else in the house. On weekdays this translated to 5:30 A.M. Settled into one particular chair, I read my Bible and then prayed for each member of our family. Although I never made a big deal about this habit, occasionally the kids would catch a glimpse of me there as they began their own busy days.

On Sunday evenings I would ask my husband and children for any particular things they'd like me to pray about that week. Such concerns as tests, projects, or schoolwork that were due, and once in awhile class bullies or teachers were voiced. (Whenever "teachers" came up, I figured my child had been given a great deal of homework and resented it.)

Often in the morning I'd find little folded notes on my prayer chair. Now that our children are raised, I wish I'd saved some of those crumpled "last-minute additions" always written on notebook paper. But I do have memories of the celebrating we did when one of those prayers was answered.

Are you laying your own requests before the Lord?

From *Daily Wisdom for Women*
BY CAROL L. FITZPATRICK

GOD'S PRECIOUS PROMISES

His divine power has granted to us
everything pertaining to life and godliness,
through the true knowledge of Him who
called us by His own glory and excellence.
For by these He has granted to us
His precious and magnificent promises,
so that by them you may become
partakers of the divine nature,
having escaped the corruption that is in the world by lust.

2 PETER 1:3–5 NASB

*F*rom the moment a baby is conceived it has everything it needs to grow into a complete human being, everything except time. For time acts as a refiner. Our spiritual growth is the same. From the moment we accept Christ, He infuses His Spirit within us, giving us right standing with the Father and making us a child of God. "He made Him who knew no sin to be sin on our behalf, so that we might become the righteousness of God in Him" (2 Corinthians 5:21 NASB). As we walk in step with Him, learning His ways, we will eventually reflect these changes in our character.

Peter reminds us that Jesus Christ is the Savior. "Therefore, brethren, be all the more diligent to make certain about His calling and choosing you; for as long as you practice these things, you will never stumble; for in this way the entrance into the eternal kingdom of our Lord and Savior Jesus Christ will be abundantly supplied to you" (2 Peter 1:10–11 NASB).

From *Daily Wisdom for Women*
BY CAROL L. FITZPATRICK

WHERE IS THE PROMISE OF HIS COMING?

Know this first of all, that in the last days
mockers will come with their mocking,
following after their own lusts, and saying,
"Where is the promise of His coming?
For ever since the fathers fell asleep,
all continues just as it was from the beginning of creation."
For when they maintain this, it escapes their notice
that by the word of God the heavens existed long ago
and the earth was formed out of water by water,
through which the world at that time was destroyed,
being flooded with water.

2 PETER 3:3–6 NASB

If you aren't into eschatology, or the study of events to come at the end of time, perhaps you won't share my appreciation of this verse. However, here's Peter, over two thousand years ago, letting us know that the earth we know will someday be destroyed. How will this happen?

"But by His word the present heavens and earth are being reserved for fire, kept for the day of judgment and destruction of ungodly men" (2 Peter 3:7 NASB).

How can a loving God destroy the very men and women and their world which He created? Look at how much time He provided for them to repent. From the time Noah received the order from God to build the ark until the rain began, a span of 120 years had elapsed. Certainly this was time enough for everyone to hear the prediction and take appropriate action.

From *Daily Wisdom for Women*
BY CAROL L. FITZPATRICK

GOD'S PROTECTION FOR WIDOWS

The LORD will tear down the house of the proud,
But He will establish the boundary of the widow.

PROVERBS 15:25 NASB

Christmas shopping preoccupied my father's thoughts as he picked out one special gift for each child, something he or she had wanted all year. But just after the last gift had been purchased, a severe heart attack overtook my dad. Although he was rushed to the hospital adjacent to the shopping center, he died almost immediately.

My mother's first concern was how she might continue caring for her children, all ten of whom lived at home.

Although she hadn't worked outside the home in years, Mom donned a beret and smock and began selling pastel portraits at the local swap meet. Eventually Mom also filled artists' chairs at Knotts Berry Farm and the Movieland Wax Museum. Her beautiful pastel portraits still hang in homes throughout our area. And the friendships she made with other artists endure to this day.

No matter what her hardships, Mom has honored God, in whom she placed her faith and the care of her life. She's now been widowed far longer than the years she was married. She's raised her children, paid off her mortgage, and passed down her love of art to all her grandchildren.

From *Daily Wisdom for Women*
BY CAROL L. FITZPATRICK

HORROR STORIES

But let all who take refuge in you be glad;
let them ever sing for joy.
Spread your protection over them,
that those who love your name may rejoice in you.

PSALM 5:11 NIV

*N*ow that our children are full grown, they're beginning to fill us in on their childhood. We always knew where they were and who they were with—or so we thought until two of them laughed about exploring the neighborhood storm drain system and traveling the pipes to sneak up on the children from the next block. Thoughts of rats and filth and sudden downpours filled me with horror. The kids then went on to tell the tale of the neighborhood boy who had almost tried to disprove the law of gravity. The stories went on and on, and my vision of being a good mother for all those years began to fade. Still, they somehow all survived and grew into perfectly normal adults—a blessing we no longer attribute to our own efforts.

No matter how vigilant parents are, they cannot possibly be everywhere, see everything, and have all the answers. Even the best of kids must try the patience of their guardian angels in their explorations of life. With the emergence of every horrifying tale our children now feel free to tell us, God's protection and love become even more real and miraculous to us. We had done a decent job, but not on our own, and we gave thanks for all those busy, patient angels that hung around for so many years.

From *Everyday Abundance*
BY TONI SORTOR

WORRY

Casting all your care upon him; for he careth for you.

1 PETER 5:7 KJV

I used to worry a lot. Thankfully, as I've become older, I've become less anxious. Besides, worry is a waste of precious time. So I don't fret as much as I used to. But when I do—I do it big.

Take the weekend Matthew went camping on short notice. When I said, "You may go," I was thinking about food, not about the dangers of camping.

Later at supper, a thought overcame me: a camping accident; Matthew would be seriously hurt—or worse.

I tried to shake the feeling but couldn't. What if he were hurt or killed? I hadn't taken his picture in months—what could I show people?

"Honey," Mike said, "are you all right?"

"No. I just had a bad feeling. Matthew is going to get hurt."

Mike, who distrusts feelings, was unmoved. "He's probably in more danger playing soccer than camping. He'll be fine. Just trust God."

Leave it to a man to derail a four-star worry! Annoyed by his logic, I left the table. Finally I prayed and the fear dissipated.

"Worry," someone told me, "is taking on a responsibility God never intended you to have."

When we worry, we think God is not able to control a situation or care for our loved ones. Worry is faithlessness; it's a sin.

Matthew came home excited—and intact.

I hugged him. And then I took his picture.

From *Lessons for a SuperMom*
BY HELEN WIDGER MIDDLEBROOKE

TRUST

Trust in the LORD, and do good;
Dwell in the land, and feed on His faithfulness.

PSALM 37:3 NKJV

He is always available, my security. He is my sustenance, my very life. As a wise parent, He gives good food suitable to His child's ability to chew and digest—just what I need, always sufficient to satisfy.

I have found peace within and a confidence that God is in control and is maintaining my cause. When the gale sweeps in with a blow that knocks the props out from under me, I have been profoundly impressed by God's audible words of peace in my heart. He gave grace to accept the "dangling" feeling, wondering what I should do next, fearing that I can't make it through this, dreading to face a life that will never be quite the same.

I just now dumped dry cereal into my bowl of ice-cold milk, but before the bowl was full, I found that I could not get any more cereal out of that box.

Life is like that—full of surprises, some pleasant, many poignant. I had already eaten enough cereal. I wasn't hungry. So it was good that the box turned up empty. God provided exactly what I most needed—control.

If the Lord Jesus does not come in the clouds today and take us out of here and into God's immediate presence, I will expect God's perfect care of me to continue for the duration. When God gives, I will find that I always possess all I have needed, and so much more!

From *All I Have Needed*
BY ELVA MINETTE MARTIN

TEACHER

Even as he walks along the road,
the fool lacks sense and shows everyone how stupid he is.

Ecclesiastes 10:3 niv

It wasn't until I tried teaching that I truly came to admire teachers. I was the worst teacher I ever met, a world-class incompetent, so I quit before anyone got wise and fired me. The kids and I had a great time, and I enjoyed being with them, but I doubt they learned anything useful.

I had never taken an education course in college because I believed they were a waste of time, and I had no intention of becoming a teacher until someone offered me the job. I had little to no patience as a teacher and spent most of that semester just trying to keep order in the classroom. What I tried to teach they had no interest in learning, and I didn't blame them in the least. They were good kids; I was a terrible teacher.

But I learned a lot. That semester was my first education in failure. What appeared to be an easy job with good hours was in no way easy. I worked hard and long and still failed—something I had never done before in my life and never expected to do. It was a good lesson in humility for a new college graduate who believed a degree could open any door. It might open doors, but it didn't guarantee success—especially when I chose the wrong door to open.

From *Everyday Abundance*
BY Toni Sortor

A FATHER TO THE FATHERLESS

A father of the fatherless and a judge for the widows,
Is God in His holy habitation.

PSALM 68:5 NASB

*B*etween the rising divorce rate and those who have chosen to birth children without benefit of marriage, over half of the households in America have become fatherless. The Christian men's movement, Promise Keepers, has sought to rectify this tragedy by calling men to refocus their priorities, first on God and then on their families.

But how about the moms? What can we do to insure that our children aren't among the fatherless? We can make sure that we are fully committed to the Lord. If you're holding down a full-time job, finding the time for Bible study and devotions is a gigantic challenge. It's up to you to get inventive.

Perhaps you can teach the children how to make their own lunches—and use that extra fifteen minutes to read the Word. This is an investment in their future growth: As you learn, so will your children.

If divorce has touched you personally, all that anger, hurt, and pain must be dealt with so that your children don't feel desolate. It's hard enough for them to lose one parent through absence, let alone the other to hostility or depression.

God has promised to be "a father to the fatherless." Count on Him to keep His Word. And instead of attempting to be both father and mother, you can just be a mom to your kids.

From *Daily Wisdom for Women*
BY CAROL L. FITZPATRICK

ALL DRIED UP

But whoso hearkeneth unto me shall dwell safely,
and shall be quiet from fear of evil.

PROVERBS 1:33 KJV

*W*hat do I need today that my Father will not or cannot provide? The answer to that question is, "Nothing!" When He planned my life, God included within His eternal purpose the supply of my every need.

One must have water; yet the brook dried up. Elijah was helpless to stop the water from disappearing. It simply evaporated into the dry air. In the same way, I am helpless to provide my own needs today. I am cast upon You, oh, Lord. By grace I will not fear, because You already know all about my need. You have planned to supply my need when I definitely need it.

There is the key: When do I need it? If I insist on being prepared well ahead of the deadline, I may indeed feel fear, because I do not know where the provision is. But if I do not actually need it right now, right this minute, then I certainly cannot accuse God of not providing my need.

It is so easy to confuse wants with actual immediate needs. Separating the two helps. God tells us in Psalm 136:25 that He gives food to all flesh. I need to recognize that "gives" is in the present tense. He constantly gives all I need right now.

From *All I Have Needed*
BY ELVA MINETTE MARTIN

BALANCING THE BUDGET

May the words of my mouth and
the meditation of my heart
be pleasing in your sight,
O Lord, my Rock and my Redeemer.

PSALM 19:14 NIV

*D*ear Father, how can I pay these bills? Sometimes I don't even know where food money will come from. I'm working as hard as possible, but on paper I can't meet the budget.

I give it to You, dear Lord. I place myself and these bills in Your hands and ask for Your direction. Show me how I can help others even while I hurt financially. Help me share a portion of my earnings with You for Your glory. Remind me to give You first place in my pocketbook!

Teach me to be prudent in my spending, wise in my financial decisions, and responsible in attempting to pay my obligations.

Enable me to trust You to provide for my needs, so I won't worry about food or drink, money or clothes. You already know my needs. I thank You for providing.

Let me not be anxious about tomorrow. I know You will take care of that, too. I will take each day as it comes and commit it to You.

I will trust You, Lord, and not lean on my own understanding of these situations. Instead, with all my might, I will recognize Your will to direct my paths.

From *When I'm on My Knees*
BY ANITA CORRINE DONIHUE

GOD'S RAVENS

For the LORD God is a sun and shield:
the LORD will give grace and glory:
no good thing will he withhold
from them that walk uprightly.

PSALM 84:11 KJV

*I*t is good to look back and remember the way that God has filled my needs. Maybe I cannot even recall all the little helps He put together to make it enough, but it was! How abundant is God's provision! He will never allow His children to lack any good thing. Always, all I have needed, God's hand has provided.

God shields from the scorching of the sun yet provides sunlight and warmth. Just so, I need the visible blessings of daily provision that God supplies without fail. I also need to be shielded from focusing on my selfish desires and from greedily clinging to the gifts God supplies as temporary provisions for this temporal life. God not only bestows with a lavish hand but also shields me from myself. When everything else is shadowed by my Shield, I look into the sunlight of His face, and all is well.

God so delights to bless His own! He says He withholds nothing at all that is good for us. All, yes, *all* I have needed, He has supplied. All I will need He will continue to supply in His perfect time—just the moment that I need it! How blessed is the one who trusts in Him!

From *All I Have Needed*
BY ELVA MINETTE MARTIN

WHISPERS IN MY EAR

*The secret of the LORD is
with them that fear him.*

PSALM 25:14 KJV

*T*he great victory on Mount Carmel was complete. God had triumphed over the prophets of Baal! Elijah fearlessly announced to King Ahab, "Get thee up, eat and drink; for there is a sound of abundance of rain" (1 Kings 18:41 KJV). God reveals His secrets to His servants who wait on Him.

First Samuel 9:15 records that the Lord, on the previous day, had told Samuel something in his ear. Think of that! A secret of God's heart was conveyed directly to a human heart in the normal way that friends share a secret: God whispered in Samuel's ear.

My God is alive! My God is my friend who walks, talks, and shares with me, and I with Him! He puts in my mind what I need to know, the direction I ought to go, and sometimes simply reminds me, "I love you so!"

Yes, the more I trust God, the more He trusts His secrets to me. The more God whispers in my ear through His Word, the more confidence I place in Him, and the more I find desire to obey Him and do fearlessly whatever He asks. In the doing, I realize God's provision, and my faith is strengthened.

How pleasant it is to hear the "whispers" of God in my ear! What wonders of sweet, satisfying companionship we share, eternal God and just me!

From *All I Have Needed*
BY ELVA MINETTE MARTIN

SHIFTING INTO OVERDRIVE

Because of the LORD'S great love we are not consumed,
for his compassions never fail.
They are new every morning;
great is your faithfulness.

LAMENTATIONS 3:22–23 NIV

*T*his is one of those hectic days, Lord, where I'm forced to shift into overdrive. I'm meeting myself coming and going. Although the things I must accomplish are good, I'm struggling to keep above all that's happening.

Even though these days are busy, thank You for helping me along the way. I tried to simplify today's schedule ahead of time, but more last-minute little things plopped in my lap. You are so wonderful for granting me a joyful heart and the energy to shift into overdrive, so I could make it through successfully.

When I feel like I'm spinning my wheels, You help me along and sometimes give me a little push. When I begin to panic and lose my focus, You remind me of Your calming, guiding presence.

I delight in Your goodness and will strive to walk (or run) in Your footsteps. When I get a little wobbly, I praise You for stabilizing me.

Thank You, Lord, for loving me and helping me relax, for minimizing my frustrations. Each time I listen to Your leading, You seem to add hours to my day.

For this day's help and guidance, I thank You, Lord. Please help tomorrow be a little less hectic so I can shift out of overdrive!

From *When I'm in His Presence*
BY ANITA CORRINE DONIHUE

A NARROW GATE

*"For the gate is small
and the way is narrow that leads to life,
and there are few who find it."*

MATTHEW 7:14 NASB

*I*t was time for me to take the written driver's license renewal test.

As the man began scoring my test I looked at the sheet in disbelief. Many of the questions I thought I'd answered correctly were wrong. In fact, I missed so many that I flunked the test. Confident that this had been a fluke, I grasped the DMV study book he extended to me. "You can retake the test, but read the book carefully," he cautioned.

Feeling in possession of the critical concepts, I returned for another test sheet. To my dismay, I flunked the test again. This time the man at the window said I'd have to wait a month to retake the test, and if I didn't pass it, a driving test would also be required. A month later I returned, having read the book from cover to cover and survived the quizzing my husband initiated. The license was finally mine. Knowing the right answers and then taking them to heart is critical in our spiritual life, as well. You can't get a driver's license without passing a test. You can't get to heaven unless you are truly born again.

From *Daily Wisdom for Women*
BY CAROL L. FITZPATRICK

BY THIS I KNOW

I am the resurrection, and the life:
he that believeth in me, though he were dead,
yet shall he live:
and whosoever liveth and believeth in me shall never die.

JOHN 11:25–26 KJV

*W*hat will it be like when Jesus takes us to heaven and says, "See, here is your loved one, perfect, and whole, and like Me!" We will be reunited in fully satisfying, never ending joy!

Then we will know with surety, without doubt, and forever that the Word of God is true! But we can trust God's Word now, even in death. He has promised. Do you believe Him?

The promise is certain for each individual—from the beginning of time until the end of it—who believes in the Lord Jesus Christ for forgiveness of sin. The house of clay, that vehicle God has provided us for living on earth, doing His will, and glorifying His name, may wear out and die. It will be left below for now. But soul and spirit will live—immediately at leaving the body and forever—in God's presence. Even the body will be resurrected and changed to fitness for life in eternity. First Corinthians 15 tells that it will be changed to be like Jesus' glorified body. Body, soul, and spirit will be reunited when Jesus comes in the Rapture to call all believers to be with Him eternally.

God alone holds the breath of life.

From *All I Have Needed*
BY ELVA MINETTE MARTIN

TOTAL CONSECRATION

Saying, Father, if thou be willing,
remove this cup from me:
nevertheless not my will, but thine, be done.

LUKE 22:42 KJV

*I*f you ask how you may know that you have truly consecrated yourself to Him, observe every indication of His will concerning you, no matter how trivial, and see whether you at once close in with that will. Lay down this principle as law—God does nothing arbitrarily. If He takes away your health, it is because He has some reason for doing so; and this is true of everything you value; and if you have real faith in Him, you will not insist on knowing the reason. If you find, in the course of daily events, that your self-consecration revolts at His will—do not be discouraged, but fly to your Savior and stay in His presence 'til you obtain the spirit in which He cried in His hour of anguish. Every time you do this it will be easier to do it; every such consent to suffer will bring you nearer and nearer to Him; and in this nearness to Him you will find such peace, such blessed, sweet peace as will make your life infinitely happy, no matter what may be its mere outside conditions. Just think of the honor and the joy of having your will one with the Divine will and so becoming changed into Christ's image from glory to glory!

ELIZABETH PRENTISS
From *A Gentle Spirit*
COMPILED BY ASHLEIGH BRYCE CLAYTON

THE GIFT OF LIFE

Every good gift and every perfect gift is from above,
and cometh down from the Father of lights.

JAMES 1:17 KJV

I would say, first of all, that this blessed life must not be looked upon in any sense as an attainment, but as an obtainment. We cannot earn it, we cannot climb up to it, we cannot win it; we can do nothing but ask for it and receive it. It is the gift of God in Christ Jesus. And where a thing is a gift, the only course left for the receiver is to take it and thank the giver. We never say of a gift, "See to what I have attained," and boast of our skill and wisdom in having attained it; but we say, "See what has been given me," and boast of the love and wealth and generosity of the giver. And everything in our salvation is a gift. From beginning to end, God is the giver and we are the receivers; and it is not to those who do great things, but to those who "receive abundance of grace and of the gift of righteousness" that the richest promises are made.

HANNAH WHITALL SMITH
From *A Gentle Spirit*
COMPILED BY ASHLEIGH BRYCE CLAYTON

WHAT THINK YE OF CHRIST?

What think ye of Christ?

MATTHEW 22:42 KJV

*T*he crucial question for each one of us in our everyday life is just this, "What think ye of Christ?" To some, the question may seem to require a doctrinal answer, and I do not at all say that there is no idea of doctrine involved in it. But to my mind, the doctrinal answer, valuable as it may be, is not the one of most importance for every day. The vital answer is the one that would contain our own personal knowledge of the character of Christ; not what He is doctrinally, but what He is intrinsically, in Himself. For, after all, our salvation does not depend upon the doctrines concerning Christ, but upon the person of Christ Himself, what He is and upon what He does.

"For the which cause I also suffer these things: nevertheless I am not ashamed: for I know whom I have believed, and am persuaded that he is able to keep that which I have committed unto him against that day" (2 Timothy 1:12).

Paul knew Christ; therefore, Paul could trust Him; and if we would trust Him as Paul did, we must know Him as intimately. I am afraid a great many people are so taken up with Christian doctrines and dogmas, and are so convinced that their salvation is secured because their "views" are sound and orthodox, that they have never yet come to a personal acquaintance with Christ Himself.

HANNAH WHITALL SMITH
From *A Gentle Spirit*
COMPILED BY ASHLEIGH BRYCE CLAYTON

WHAT FELLOWSHIP IS THIS?

Elias was a man subject to
like passions as we are.

JAMES 5:17 KJV

ubject to like passions as we are" is what James offers as a description of Elijah of the Old Testament. Elijah experienced the same feelings and affections we experience. It is safe to deduce that he feared, hesitated, doubted, and dreaded. He walked on with God and learned to appropriate God's presence and peace, power and persistence. He also claimed God's answers to his prayers uttered by the word of heart desire.

When it comes to the prayer of faith, we must look up and ask God for delight in Him that will not entertain doubt. Such faith only comes through knowing God personally, seeking His heart, receiving from Him the burden for specific requests, and depending totally upon Him. As He enables, we can boldly pray in Jesus' name. Faith will not fail to receive, for it is God Himself who promised to answer such prayer.

The Scripture says Elijah prayed in earnestness. He was fervent and persevered in prayer. He did not suddenly find himself in need, look up, and say: "God, I am Elijah, and am I glad to meet You, because I hear that You will dole out whatever I need right now."

Elijah obviously had come to catch the ear of God! The eternal God was Elijah's God. Elijah had believed on Him. Though he was a man of like passions with us, Elijah asked and received from the God of heaven and earth!

From *All I Have Needed*
BY ELVA MINETTE MARTIN

AN INFLEXIBLE WILL

*For it is God who works in you to will
and to act according to his good purpose.*

PHILIPPIANS 2:13 NIV

*I*t has been said "that a fixed, inflexible will is a great assistance in a holy life."

You can will to use every means of grace appointed by God.

You can will to spend much time in prayer without regard to your frame at the moment.

You can will to prefer a religion of principle to one of mere feeling; in other words, to obey the will of God when no comfortable glow of emotion accompanies your obedience.

You cannot will to possess the spirit of Christ; that must come as His gift; but you can choose to study His life and imitate it. This will infallibly lead to such self-denying work as visiting the poor, nursing the sick, giving of your time and money to the needy, and the like.

If the thought of such self-denial is repugnant to you, remember that it is enough for the disciple to be as his Lord. And let me assure you that as you penetrate the labyrinth of life in pursuit of Christian duty, you will often be surprised and charmed by meeting your Master Himself amid its windings and turnings and receive His soul-inspiring smile. Or, I should rather say, you will always meet Him, wherever you go.

ELIZABETH PRENTISS
From *A Gentle Spirit*
COMPILED BY ASHLEIGH BRYCE CLAYTON

DEALING WITH ANNOYING PEOPLE

Judge not according to the appearance,
but judge righteous judgment.

JOHN 7:24 KJV

*Y*ou forget perhaps the indirect good one may gain by living with uncongenial, tempting persons. . .such people do good by the very self-denial and self-control their mere presence demands.

"But suppose one cannot exercise self-control and is always flying out and flaring up?"

"I should say that a Christian who was always doing that. . . was in pressing need of just the trial God sent.

"It is very mortifying and painful to find how weak one is."

"That is true. But our mortifications are some of God's best physicians and do much toward healing our pride and self-conceit."

"We look at our fellow men too much from the standpoint of our own prejudices. They may be wrong, they may have their faults and foibles, they may call out all the meanest and most hateful in us. But when they excite our bad passions by their own, they may be as ashamed and sorry as we are irritated. And I think some of the best, most contrite, most useful of men and women, whose prayers prevail with God and bring down blessings into the homes in which they dwell, often possess unlovely traits that furnish them with their best discipline. The very fact that they are ashamed of themselves drives them to God; they feel safe in His presence."

ELIZABETH PRENTISS
From *A Gentle Spirit*
COMPILED BY ASHLEIGH BRYCE CLAYTON

BEING A MASTERPIECE

"My grace is sufficient for you,
for my power is made perfect in weakness."

2 CORINTHIANS 12:9 NIV

*H*e can take the broken pieces of any life and create out of them a work of art that will bring glory to Him and blessing to others. He can take even the wounds dealt to you by both circumstances and others and use them for His glory. So long as you put yourself in God's hands, nothing can keep Him from turning your life into the beautiful creation He always intended it to be.

No matter what you are today—or what you were in the past—you are not a mistake. You are a potential work of art in which God wants to reveal His power, glory, love, and creativity. God can take your suffering and turn it into a blessing for yourself and others. Don't hold a grudge against God. Let Him work with you as you are and turn your life into the masterpiece He has planned for it.

The first step in seeing yourself as God sees you—as a person of worth and value—is to take a look at the canvas on which He wants to create this masterpiece, so you can understand who you are. When you understand just who you truly are, you'll have a clearer idea of what God's perspective on your life really is.

From *Created for a Purpose*
BY DARLENE SALA

THE BODY OF CHRIST

In fact God has arranged the parts
in the body, every one of them,
just as he wanted them to be.
If they were all one part,
where would the body be?
As it is, there are many parts,
but one body.

1 CORINTHIANS 12:18–20 NIV

The apostle Paul understood the way people think. He knew they would be comparing themselves to each other, wondering why they couldn't have the same gifts and abilities that someone else had. He understood that people's self-esteem would all too often be wounded as they looked around the church at the many talented and outstanding people.

To help heal these wounds, Paul used a human body as his illustration. When we look at another person and think, *She's so much more outgoing than I am, so she must be worth more to God,* that makes as much sense as it would if your foot got all upset because it couldn't be your hand. Or if we look at a gifted leader and think, *Compared to her, I'm nothing, so I might just as well give up,* that's as silly as if your ear started crying because it couldn't be an eye.

The point Paul is making is this: We all need each other. Your hand is just as dependent on your eye as your eye is on your hand— and your head needs your feet as much as your feet need your head. We are all part of the body that is the Church.

From *Created for a Purpose*
BY DARLENE SALA

156

MY CHURCH FAMILY

And let us consider how we may spur one another
on toward love and good deeds.
Let us not give up meeting together,
as some are in the habit of doing,
but let us encourage one another.

HEBREWS 10:24–25 NIV

Father, I'm grateful to You for giving me my church family. I stand back and watch as they bustle about, always looking for ways to encourage one another. I can never keep up with the blessings I receive from my church family, the family of God.

When advice is needed, they are quick to listen and slow to offer opinions. When advice is given, it is fruitful, like shiny apples in a finely woven basket.

Brothers and sisters in Christ often share and encourage each other in God's love. Tiny clusters of believers form, holding up needs in prayer. Cards and letters with encouraging words heal the downtrodden. True, growing believers never put one another down.

Thank You for the example they set for our young people and new Christians. Thank You for caution shown in lives so no one is caused to stumble. Thank You for older people "adopting" younger couples, for the younger watching out for the elderly. For prayers and praises given for each other, I am so thankful. Bless these helpers and prayer warriors, dear Lord.

Thank You for my priceless church family.

From *When I'm Praising God*
BY ANITA CORRINE DONIHUE

JESUS' LOVE

"For God so loved the world
that he gave his one and only Son,
that whoever believes in him
shall not perish but have eternal life."

JOHN 3:16 NIV

*W*e get so caught up in looking at life from our limited, human perspective that we become blind to what is real. The Bible tells us that God values us so much that He gave His only Son so that we can live forever. That's how valuable we are, now and forever.

So compared to that eternal and awesome truth, our own estimations of value don't amount to much. I may not have the face or figure that would ever launch a thousand ships—but who cares? God loves me. I may not be gifted or talented—but what difference does that make? God thought I was worth the price of His only Son. My relationships may all seem like failures right now, and my house is shabby and rundown, and I hate my clothes—but how can that possibly compare to the knowledge that God loves me so much He wants me to live with Him forever?

Over and over the New Testament tells us the same message: Jesus loves us so much He gave His life for us.

From *Created for a Purpose*
BY DARLENE SALA

WHERE AM I GOING?

*"I [Jesus] will come back and take you to be with me
that you also may be where I am."*

JOHN 14:2–3 NIV

This question is the scariest to the nonbeliever and the most wonderful to one who trusts in Christ. When life is over, if I have a personal relationship with Jesus, I am going to be with God.

Some days we may feel proud of what we have to offer God—but other days we'll feel pretty embarrassed about what we have to give Him. But God really doesn't care either way. He just wants us to lay our lives on His altar.

Do you have a quick temper? Give it to God. Are you clumsy? Put your clumsiness in God's hand. Are you overweight? Offer your body to God as a living sacrifice. God doesn't want just the "good stuff." He wants it all. He will use it all, good and bad, for His kingdom.

Some day we are going to be with the Lord forever and ever. I'm convinced that only in heaven will we know the unseen ways in which God has used us to bless those around us and accomplish His purposes. Trust Him to use your life—all of it—as a tool of value in His eternal design.

From *Created for a Purpose*
BY DARLENE SALA

GOD'S PURPOSE

*I press on to take hold of that for which
Christ Jesus took hold of me.*

PHILIPPIANS 3:12 NIV

After his conversion, I'm sure Satan must have tried to keep Paul fixed on the past, wallowing in shame and regret over all the horrible things he had done.

Sometimes we would like to live in the past, back when we were younger and prettier and stronger, when people we loved were still with us and needed us, when we felt competent and more in control of our lives. But God doesn't want us to live in the past. Whether the past was bad or good, God wants us to press on.

God understands how weak we really are. While challenging us in Matthew 5:48 to be mature or complete, He provides a way for us when we fall short: confession and forgiveness. "If we confess our sins, he is faithful and just and will forgive us our sins and purify us from all unrighteousness" (1 John 1:9 NIV).

Our goal in life should not be to pursue what the world says is valuable but to strive to be what God says is valuable. We should endeavor to take hold not of someone else's reason for being, but of God's purpose for us. I do not have to place a price tag on my value. My job is to press toward the mark of God's purpose and leave the rest to Him.

From *Created for a Purpose*
BY DARLENE SALA

ITCH

" 'I will heal my people
and will let them enjoy
abundant peace and security.' "

JEREMIAH 33:6 NIV

*M*y husband is recovering from shoulder surgery. He should not move the shoulder for two weeks, so the doctor gave him a harness that makes it impossible for the shoulder to move. All in all, he's making great progress, even though he's bored to death. His main complaint is that everything itches. His stitches itch; the skin under the harness itches; the beard he's growing because he can't shave left-handed itches. We use lotions and powders, but still he itches. It's driving us both crazy. The cat that sleeps on my husband's stomach is not happy, either, because my husband itches in his sleep.

The itching is the least of all possible problems, of course. The surgery might not have done the job. He may not be able to fish all summer. He can't drive. He faces weeks of physical therapy, and he starts a new job as soon as the stitches come out. But these worries don't bother him too much because he has the itching to complain about. In a weird way the itching is a blessing, something that takes his mind off more serious concerns. God knows how easily we humans are distracted and sometimes places irritating but harmless annoyances between us and more serious developments until we are strong enough to deal with them. For now, it's good that he itches.

From *Everyday Abundance*
BY TONI SORTOR

THROUGH LITTLE EYES

*From the lips of
children and infants
you have ordained praise.*

PSALM 8:2 NIV

*B*efore each child entered the crawl-around stage, I would crawl on all fours to "childproof" our home. As the girls have grown, I've realized that babyhood isn't the only time that it's important to look through a child's eyes.

Sometimes we moms are so busy that we forget our children have quite a lot to teach us—if we'll take the time to learn. Quite often what seems ordinary to us becomes spectacular from a child's perspective.

My friend Holly and her daughter were admiring a full moon when Mary Cate announced with three-year-old wonder, "Look, Mama, the moon has all its pieces!" With a smile and a hug, the moment was sealed in that mother's heart for all time.

Children remind us to laugh, no—giggle. They help us rediscover the simple joys of the sun on our face and grass under bare feet.

But even more important, children teach us about God. They show us how to pray believing and how to live abundantly. They take their heavenly Father at His word, and they expect us to do the same.

What happiness God must feel when His little messengers reach the heart of an adult! For surely He is pleased when we remember to take joy in loving Him, in just being His child.

From *Time Out*
BY LEIGH ANN THOMAS

A RARE JEWEL

Let us not become weary in doing good,
for at the proper time we will reap a harvest
if we do not give up.

GALATIANS 6:9 NIV

I proudly gazed at sixteen-year-old Michelle as she helped a group of our Church School children memorize Bible verses. Her long blond hair fell softly forward when she bent close with a listening ear. A shy little girl with clasped hands behind her back whispered her newly learned verse. Afterward, Michelle praised her for a job well done.

The first time I met Michelle was when she started coming to our church about two years ago. I almost could see "leadership" printed right across her forehead.

It wasn't long until Michelle accepted my invitation to help me in Bible Explorer's Club. The program is built on individualized Bible memorization, so I'm always grateful for assistance.

I was delighted to discover that Michelle had studied the same program as a child. She jumped right in like it was second nature.

Last Christmas Michelle accepted the job of directing our children's Christmas program. She rewrote the script, recruited faithful helpers, and produced a successful program for us all to enjoy.

Michelle has many wonderful abilities far beyond her years. But the one that shines above them all is her commitment to faithfulness. We have all seen people who possess the abilities—but if you can't depend upon them, none of that matters. Keeping a promise is important to Michelle, a marvelous attribute for a teenage girl.

She is a rare jewel. I love her and appreciate her. Thank you, Michelle, for your faithfulness.

From *When I'm Praising God*
BY ANITA CORRINE DONIHUE

HEARTS ENTWINED FOREVER

Above all, love each other deeply.

1 PETER 4:8 NIV

*W*hen my daughter Emily was little, she was my constant companion. Her little chattering voice brought new life to everything I did. Once, waiting in an examination room, the two of us were talking a blue streak when the nurse came in. "You two are best buddies, aren't you?" she said. And we were.

When Emily went to preschool, I gave her a gold heart of mine to wear, to remind her that my love went with her. When I went into the hospital for the birth of my second child, she gave it back to remind me that her love would be with me. And when she went to kindergarten, I bought her a duplicate necklace, so that she would know she was always in my heart.

But as she grew older and my life got busier, I sometimes worried that I would lose her, that she would disappear into her own new world of school and friends, and I would never recover the person who had been such a good companion to me.

As she becomes a young woman instead of a child, I find we relate to each other in a new way. Now, as we have woman-to-woman talks, I realize she's still a good companion. And yesterday, as she was hurrying off to meet her friends, I noticed the small gold heart that glittered at her throat. I touched the gold heart around my own neck and smiled.

From *Just the Girls*
BY ELLYN SANNA

LEARNING TO LET GO

"And underneath are the everlasting arms."

DEUTERONOMY 33:27 NIV

*D*arla and Sam struggled to raise their three teenagers the right way. Although the parents loved the Lord, their efforts seemed futile. Their kids were breaking away from Christian teachings and heading for a life of disaster.

Darla felt devastated. She tried to hang onto them, bridging the gap (she thought) between them and God, one hand gripping God's and the other, her children.

One night after an argument, Darla stumbled to her bedroom and fell to her knees. Between sobs she revealed her broken heart to God.

"I can't lose my kids from You, Lord." She pounded the bed with her fists. "What more can I do?"

God's Spirit ministered to Darla with His love. He asked who came first, Him or her children? Would she be willing to go to heaven with or without them? He told Darla to keep loving her kids, but to let them go. One by one Darla released her grip on her kids. She stood, feeling victory and relief. Then she realized when she finally let go, God was there to catch them in His everlasting arms. She had freed Him to work directly in their lives. Until then, she had been standing between them and the Lord.

Soon after, the children grew closer to Him. Now Darla and Sam thank the Lord for His help.

From *When I'm on My Knees*
BY ANITA CORRINE DONIHUE

OUR TEENAGE CHILDREN

Train a child in the way he should go,
and when he is old
he will not turn from it.

PROVERBS 22:6 NIV

The music, hair, and clothes have changed, Lord. The children within have not. One day our teenagers feel one way, the next day it's entirely different. I feel like a yo-yo on roller skates!

Thank You for being with us through the joys and tears, for promising me that as we train up our children in the way of God, they will not depart from You.

Thank You for helping me never compromise the standards You have set for me. I praise You for cautioning me to be kind and generous, honest and open, clean-minded and wise in speech.

When our precious teens rebel, I praise You for help and protection for them. Thank You for being their Good Shepherd. During the times I can't seem to do anything right in their eyes, I cling to You for guidance, comfort, and reassurance.

You remind me that during these rebellious times, our teens are trying to find their own way. Thank You for helping me let go so they may search out their own personal relationship with You, so You can deal directly with them and lead them in the ways You want them to go. You, not I, are the Lord of their lives.

I marvel at the wondrous miracles You perform in each of these teenagers' lives. I praise and thank You for all You do.

From *When I'm Praising God*
BY ANITA CORRINE DONIHUE

THE REBELLIOUS CHILD

Above all, love each other deeply,
because love covers over a multitude of sins.

1 PETER 4:8 NIV

*F*ather, help my rebelling child. I am overwhelmed with worry. Will my dear one's mistakes cause a lifetime of suffering?

Forgive me, O Lord, for the wrongs I have caused my dear child. Let me humble myself and ask this loved one's forgiveness. Let me offer no excuses. Cleanse my heart from bitterness and give me a pure, unconditional love. Grant me wisdom. Teach me when to be lenient, when to be firm. Help me that my motives will be pure, honest, and aboveboard. Remind me often not to try fixing things.

Place Your angels about my child. Protect from sin and harm, and lead to Your perfect will. Soften our hearts. Give us both a hunger to love and serve You.

Now, dear Lord, I release control of my beloved child to You. I will trust You in every situation and timing. Even when I don't understand why, still will I trust and praise You. Through these troublesome times I know You are helping and keeping my dear one in Your care.

Thank You for victories to come. Thank You for hearing my prayers. Thank You that You can go places with my child that I can't. Praise You, O God, for Your mighty works. In You I put my total trust.

From *When I'm on My Knees*
BY ANITA CORRINE DONIHUE

THE WISE OF HEART

The wise of heart will receive commands,
But a babbling fool will be ruined.
He who walks in integrity walks securely,
But he who perverts his ways will be found out.

PROVERBS 10:8–9 NASB

For years James Dobson, president of Focus on the Family, has warned parents about the pitfalls ahead for their strong-willed children. Personally, we raised our three kids with one hand on the radio and the other on the Bible. Dr. Dobson's radio ministry has given us hope and kept us sane.

My repeated prayer for all our children was this: "Lord, protect them and surround them with Your angels. And if they're disobedient, let them be found out."

Years into their teens, our kids were convinced that I had spies stationed all over the city. No matter what they did, I knew about it within hours. And I can assure you, it was a direct result of this prayer.

God provided such excellent guidance for us, He entrusted eight other children into our care who were not our own. These young people were just kids who needed special care along the way. We tended to their physical needs as well as their spiritual ones. We stressed honesty and obedience and showered them with unconditional love. And each of them grew to a more secure emotional place.

Is there a young person in your life who needs your prayers today?

From *Daily Wisdom for Women*
BY CAROL L. FITZPATRICK

DIFFICULT QUESTIONS

The just shall live by faith.

GALATIANS 3:11 KJV

*O*ne morning, I was quietly sitting in my office when my son burst in.

One look and I knew a Difficult Question was coming.

"I didn't finish my quiet time," he said. "Is it okay to pray while I walk the dog?"

Whew! At last, an easy one.

"Paul said, 'pray without ceasing,' " I said. "It's okay to pray while you walk the dog. And the way your dog walks, it's highly advisable."

My son is struggling with his understanding of God. Because God is too big for him to grasp, he tends to look at and respond to just one part of Him at a time.

For example, if the Bible says we should "rise up early" to pray, then he's going to rise up early and pray. And if he fails to get up early, or falls asleep during prayer, then he thinks he has failed God and God will "get him" for it.

But God is not like that.

God is a loving, infinite, patient God. He is not a divine score-keeper. God is not some cosmic killjoy who is just waiting for us to mess up so He can give us "what we deserve."

Certainly, God wants obedience, but it's an obedience of a cheerful heart happily following where the Father leads, not a dutiful obedience to a set of rigid rules and regulations.

I pray someday my son will understand this.

It will make all of his Difficult Questions easier.

From *Lessons for a SuperMom*
BY HELEN WIDGER MIDDLEBROOKE

"I DO"

Thou art snared with the words of thy mouth.

PROVERBS 6:2 KJV

Truth be told, I never said, "I do."

I was one of those "free spirits" who insisted on writing my own vows. I was, after all, a writer. Surely I could come up with something more meaningful than the trite "for richer, for poorer."

And I did, at least I thought I did.

But those were the days before videotape, and someone forgot to turn on the cassette recorder. So if anyone, including Mike, asks what I pledged back then, I really cannot say.

Maybe those old lines are not so trite after all. Those who have said them can at least remember what they vowed to do.

The traditional vows are certainly pithy and all encompassing. I can't think of any situations in marriage not covered by the "for better for worse, for richer for poorer, in sickness and in health" umbrella.

The old vows also set a high moral standard. When everyone vowed to be committed " 'til death do us part," divorces were less common. Modern marriage services often eliminate that phrase or replace it with a loophole: "as long as our love shall last."

Some might say the words really don't matter. They'd say I'm just as married as I would have been reciting traditional ones.

But am I?

Words have meaning and consequences. They "snare" us.

When it comes to marriage vows, we'd all do well to be caught in the same trap.

From *Lessons for a SuperMom*
BY HELEN WIDGER MIDDLEBROOKE

I RESOLVE

He will be the sure foundation for your times,

ISAIAH 33:6 NIV

It's hard to believe we are standing on the threshold of a brand-new year. With excitement and anticipation I draw a deep breath and boldly take a first step into the future. I don't get very far, however, before I'm interrupted with that age-old, irritating question: "So, what's your New Year's resolution?"

Oh, good grief. Can't I just be happy about a new year without having to resolve something? Okay, I'll play along. I resolve. . .I resolve. . .I resolve to be more decisive. . .I guess. I'll clean out the refrigerator more often. Although personally, I think the moldy stuff in the back is very educational.

I'll try to remember to open the damper before I build a fire. I promise never, ever again to accidentally wash my red sweatshirt along with everyone's underwear. And I resolve most solemnly to never again use Roy's pliers to nail something on the wall (unless I can't find the hammer).

I'll try not to use the instant cash machine quite so often (unless I run out of checks). Oh, and I'll do better about recording in the check register the checks I do write. And I'll definitely put a stop to my impulse buying—unless, of course, it's on sale, wherein I declare the previous resolution null and void.

Wow. That's a lot of changes to make in one year. Maybe I should just concentrate on one or two. . . .

From *Time Out*
BY LEIGH ANN THOMAS

A TIME TO MOURN

There is an appointed time for everything.
And there is a time for every event under heaven. . .
A time to weep and a time to laugh;
A time to mourn and a time to dance.

ECCLESIASTES 3:1, 4 NASB

*O*nce we've finally accepted that God truly loves us, it's hard to face the first discouraging episode or tragedy that follows. One young family had received a strong call from the Lord to the mission field. At the beginning of a fund-raising trip they were involved in an accident that totaled their van. What would they do? They transferred their focus away from the problem and to their faithful Lord who never disappoints.

Somehow we reach the faulty conclusion that if God loves us all negative incidents are nixed. Do we doubt that the Father loved the Son and yet allowed the Son to suffer a cruel death on the cross? The penalty for sin was death, a penalty that had to be paid by someone absolutely sinless in order for us to be forgiven. Only Jesus Christ could fill that role.

If Christ Himself suffered, then why should we be immune from all maladies?

Occasionally a time of mourning enters our lives, sometimes stealing in almost silently, sometimes brashly breaking down the door to our well-constructed sense of security. Neither path reflects nor distorts the fact that God loves us. But tragedy and mourning are both part of the ebb and flow or "rhythm of life."

From *Daily Wisdom for Women*
BY CAROL L. FITZPATRICK

TRIALS HAVE A PURPOSE

Then Joseph said to his brothers,
"Please come closer to me."
And they came closer.
And he said,
"I am your brother Joseph,
whom you sold into Egypt.
Now do not be grieved or angry with yourselves,
because you sold me here,
for God sent me before you to preserve life."

GENESIS 45:4–5 NASB

How many of us could forgive as Joseph did? His jealous siblings had kidnaped him, thrown him into a pit, and then allowed him to be sold into slavery. Yet Joseph trusted that from God's perspective, not his own, his trials had a purpose.

Joseph walked through his humiliating ordeal with his eyes focused on the Lord. He continued not only to love his brothers but to find forgiveness in his heart for them. Studying his life has enabled me to look at my own situation differently: God can accomplish miracles in the midst of trials.

Is there a hurt so deep inside that you have never shared it with another human being? Perhaps someone in your own family has rejected or betrayed you. Remember the pain suffered by Joseph; remember the anguish of Jesus Christ, who was betrayed by one as close as a brother, Judas Iscariot. God knows your pain, and He is strong enough to remove any burden.

From *Daily Wisdom for Women*
BY CAROL L. FITZPATRICK

COMFORT IN MOURNING

And God shall wipe away all tears from their eyes.

REVELATION 21:4 KJV

*I*ve lost my loved one, dear Lord. I thought I would be prepared, but how could I possibly be ready for something like this? There are no more chances to share our feelings and retrieve the time, to do and say the things undone. My heart aches.

How I praise You for comfort and strength in my time of grief. Little by little, layer by layer, You are healing my heart and soul. I praise You for surrounding me with Your warm, constant presence that helps fill the void within me.

Thank You, Lord, for reminding me in Your Word about life everlasting. Because I know my dear one loved You, all isn't final. Someday You will wipe away all my tears. There will be no sickness or pain, no sin or hurt feelings. All of this will be gone, never to return!

Even though I have tears and heartache now, I thank You for Your promise that joy will come in the morning.

I realize now You are showing me it isn't my loved one I'm weeping for. It's me. Thank You, God, for Your comfort. I look forward to joining You in heaven someday and being with my loved one again. In the meantime, I know I have more to do for You here, Lord, so I will keep going on. I will serve and praise You with all my heart.

From *When I'm Praising God*
BY ANITA CORRINE DONIHUE

A VACATION FROM AFFLICTION

All the days of the afflicted are evil:
but he that is of a merry heart hath a continual feast.

PROVERBS 15:15 KJV

Things go wrong from time to time: Pets die; children rebel; money is hard to come by. One problem is enough to turn us into grouches, while problem on top of problem really makes us feel afflicted. What did we do to deserve all this? When every day becomes a burden, how can we have a "merry heart" and a "continual feast"?

I personally use the "But" technique. I have a miserable cold and an impossible deadline at work, but there are two lonely daffodils blooming at my back door that need to be admired and cherished. Our furnace died, and a late-season snowstorm is due, but there's a good fire in the fireplace and food in the pantry. My husband may lose his job, but right now our grandchildren are happily building a fortress on the floor with his help.

This is not ignoring our problems. They will still exist after we admire the daffodils, but they may not hurt quite as much. It's more like taking a short vacation from troubles, finding some little blessings to enjoy in the face of tragedy. We can't smile and frown at the same time, so it's best to smile whenever possible. Sometimes it's not easy finding the little blessings, but they are still there waiting for us if we only open our hearts and minds to them.

From *Everyday Abundance*
BY TONI SORTOR

SORROWS AND HOLY LIVING

For godly sorrow worketh repentance
to salvation not to be repented of:
but the sorrow of the world worketh death.

2 CORINTHIANS 7:10 KJV

*D*oesn't it seem hard when you think of the many there are in the world, that you should be singled out for such bereavement and loneliness?"

She replied with a smile:

"I am not singled out, dear. There are thousands of God's own dear children scattered over the world suffering far more than I do. And I do not think there are many persons in it who are happier than I am. I was bound to my God and Savior before I knew a sorrow, it is true. But it was by a chain of many links; and every link that dropped away brought me closer to Him, 'til at last, having nothing left, I was shut up to Him and learned fully what I had only learned partially, how soul-satisfying He is."

"You think, then," I said while my heart died within me, "that husband and children are obstacles in our way and hinder our getting nearer to Christ?"

"Oh no!" she cried. "God never gives us hindrances. On the contrary, He means, in making us wives and mothers, to put us into the very conditions of holy living."

ELIZABETH PRENTISS
From *A Gentle Spirit*
COMPILED BY ASHLEIGH BRYCE CLAYTON

A DISCERNING WOMAN

*Wisdom reposes in the heart of the discerning
and even among fools she lets herself be known.*

PROVERBS 14:33 NIV

*D*orothy, a precious older woman, faithfully attended my Bible study group each week despite the fact that she suffered from congestive heart failure. She was the kind of person one treasured as a gift, knowing the time with her would be all too brief. She shared the contents of her heart freely, no longer restricted behind the confining walls of decorum. From her perspective, the word "cherish" didn't exist in her husband's vocabulary.

We would pray and cry together over the grief her marriage had caused her soul. And then she'd sit and play a beautiful hymn on the piano. This is the way the Lord ministered to her pain. Confident of her eternal destination, she exuded serenity, wisdom, peace, and love. And the Lord called her home that year because He valued her tremendously. She's buried in a cemetery near my house, and I smile when I pass by, knowing she's found a refuge where the music never stops and people never cry.

Today's proverb says that "wisdom reposes in the heart of the discerning." How well Dorothy understood this. And although she couldn't change her husband's heart, her own was filled with wisdom. She'd learned the art of holding life like a kite, giving it enough room to float freely and then watching as it returned to her.

From *Daily Wisdom for Women*
BY CAROL L. FITZPATRICK

GROWING IN CHRIST

Consider the lilies how they grow.

LUKE 12:27 KJV

$\mathcal{W}$hat we all need is to "consider the flowers of the field," and learn their secret. Grow, by all means, dear Christians; but grow, I beseech you in God's way, which is the only effectual way. See to it that you are planted in grace, and then let the Divine Husbandman cultivate you in His own way and by His own means. Put yourselves out in the sunshine of His presence, and let the dew of heaven come down upon you, and see what will be the result. Leaves and flowers and fruit must surely come in their season; for your Husbandman is skillful, and He never fails in His harvesting. Only see to it that you oppose no hindrance to the shining of the Sun of Righteousness, or the falling of the dew from heaven. The thinnest covering may serve to keep off the sunshine and the dew, and the plant may wither, even where these are most abundant. And so also the slightest barrier between your soul and Christ may cause you to dwindle and fade, as a plant in a cellar or under a bushel. Keep the sky clear. Open wide every avenue of your being to receive the blessed influences your Divine Husbandman may bring to bear upon you. Bask in the sunshine of His love. Drink of the waters of His goodness. Keep your face upturned to Him as the flowers do to the sun. Look, and your soul shall live and grow.

HANNAH WHITALL SMITH
From *A Gentle Spirit*
COMPILED BY ASHLEIGH BRYCE CLAYTON

YIELD, TRUST, OBEY

Neither yield ye your members
as instruments of unrighteousness unto sin:
but yield yourselves unto God.

ROMANS 6:13 KJV

To yield anything means simply to give that thing to the care and keeping of another. To yield ourselves to the Lord, therefore, is to give ourselves to Him, giving Him the entire possession and control of our whole being. It means to abandon ourselves, to take hands off of ourselves. The word "consecration" is often used to express this yielding, but I hardly think it is a good substitute. With many people, to consecrate themselves seems to convey the idea of doing something very self-sacrificing, and very good and grand; and it therefore admits of a subtle form of self-glorification. But "yielding" conveys a far more humbling idea; it implies helplessness and weakness, and the glorification of another rather than of ourselves.

Yielding is not the idea of sacrifice, in the sense we usually give to that word, namely, as of a great cross taken up; but it is the sense of surrender, of abandonment, of giving up the control and keeping and use of ourselves unto the Lord. To yield to God means to belong to God, and to belong to God means to have all His infinite power and infinite love engaged on our side. Therefore, when I invite you to yield yourselves to Him, I am inviting you to avail yourselves of an inexpressible and most amazing privilege.

HANNAH WHITALL SMITH
From *A Gentle Spirit*
COMPILED BY ASHLEIGH BRYCE CLAYTON

ALL IS VANITY!

The words of the Preacher,
the son of David, king in Jerusalem.
"Vanity of vanities," says the Preacher,
"Vanity of vanities! All is vanity."

ECCLESIASTES 1:1–2 NASB

At the end of his life, King Solomon, who is thought to be the writer of Ecclesiastes, concludes that the things of earth are but fleeting. Perhaps you, too, are prone to reflect on the tasks which occupy your days, concluding that nothing gets accomplished.

From the very beginning my husband and I decided that I would stay home with the kids and he'd work to support us. We have always managed to own a home in a nice neighborhood, send our kids to good schools, and afford at least a summer "camping vacation."

At times I'd lust after the sumptuous decor of a neighbor's home or envy those who lived in the two-story homes in the adjacent tract. But we stayed put. Years later, I finally appreciated that "low mortgage" when we were able to refinance and send three kids to college.

As we go through Ecclesiastes, Solomon repeatedly uses two key word pictures, "meaningless" and "under the sun." As king over Israel he had seen "all the works which have been done under the sun, and behold, all is vanity and striving after wind. . . . Because in much wisdom there is much grief, and increasing knowledge results in increasing pain" (Ecclesiastes 1:14, 18 NASB). Solomon had experienced the best the world has to offer. . .and it wasn't enough.

From *Daily Wisdom for Women*
BY CAROL L. FITZPATRICK

SEEK WISDOM, NOT SELF

When a wicked man comes, contempt also comes,
And with dishonor comes scorn.

PROVERBS 18:3 NASB

The delightful movie *Doctor Doolittle* presented a magical animal called the "Push me, pull you." Such is the woman who has a divided heart! She can never truly go forward in life.

One young woman whom I counseled certainly fit this description. She'd fallen in love with a worthless wretch of a man and become convinced that she somehow possessed the power to change him. Not only could she not change him, she was also unable to raise her children properly. Because this mother was emotionally paralyzed, her children never received godly examples of faith, integrity, and stability.

Women become vulnerable the instant truth is replaced with desire. It's like when the tip of an arrow finds the one small point of vulnerability and penetrates a suit of armor.

So how can we teach our daughters to be wise? By acquiring knowledge ourselves. As we study and store God's Word in times of peace, our first thoughts during periods of stress or crisis will be Scripture. People falter because they fail to plan. If we just do what God expects of us, despite the magnetic pull of sin, we gain strength of character. Negotiating with evil nets us a zero every time.

From *Daily Wisdom for Women*
BY CAROL L. FITZPATRICK

WISDOM CALLS OUT

Does not wisdom call,
And understanding lift up her voice?
On top of the heights beside the way,
Where the paths meet, she takes her stand;
Beside the gates, at the opening to the city,
At the entrance of the doors, she cries out:
"To you, O men, I call. . .
For wisdom is better than jewels;
And all desirable things cannot compare with her."

PROVERBS 8:1–4, 11 NASB

Dream books, that's what my grandmother called catalogs. When I was young we'd view them together, imagining that we'd buy all sorts of jewels and trinkets. As I grew older I realized that none of those things we had circled really meant anything to Granny. This wise woman valued people, giving generously of her time to anyone in need.

Although she never went to college, Granny had a natural wisdom about people, an understanding of their hearts, that doesn't come from most books. Her wisdom came from knowing and living out the precepts in one book, the Bible, God's Word.

Wisdom calls to all of us, but some of us are just better listeners. Notice in this passage that wisdom is found "on top of the heights beside the way, Where the paths meet. . . ." Wisdom is a choice. We can walk right past it.

Wisdom is also "beside the gates, at the opening to the city, at the entrance of the doors. . . ." Wisdom is at the very precipice of every decision.

From *Daily Wisdom for Women*
BY CAROL L. FITZPATRICK

SEEKING WISDOM

To receive instruction in wise behavior,
Righteousness, justice and equity;
To give prudence to the naive,
To the youth knowledge and discretion,
A wise man will hear and increase in learning,
And a man of understanding will acquire wise counsel,
To understand a proverb and a figure,
The words of the wise and their riddles.

PROVERBS 1:3–6 NASB

*W*hen asked by God what he wished for, Solomon answered, "Wisdom." Looking back over your life, if you'd been afforded this same opportunity in your early twenties, what would your response have been?

Like most of us, at that age wisdom probably wasn't high on your priority list. Instead of asking God or your parents for direction, you more likely turned to your peers.

Natalie, a strikingly beautiful girl who'd just turned seventeen, found the advances of an older man extremely difficult to resist. Disregarding all the precepts she'd learned from years of Sunday school, Natalie turned instead to a non-Christian girlfriend for advice. "Go for it!" the friend encouraged with gusto.

A decade later that friend has been married and divorced. Natalie herself found out too late that her "boyfriend" already had a wife and baby.

Satan may be out of the Garden, but he still finds his way into vulnerable areas of our lives. But God is with you, even in times of sinful temptation. He's promised to give you the power to withstand such moral crises.

From *Daily Wisdom for Woman*
BY CAROL L. FITZPATRICK

TURN YOUR EAR TO WISDOM

For the LORD gives wisdom;
From His mouth come knowledge and understanding.
He stores up sound wisdom for the upright;
He is a shield to those who walk in integrity,
Guarding the paths of justice,
And He preserves the way of His godly ones.

PROVERBS 2:6–8 NASB

*E*very family has at least one relative who cannot get his act together. (Meanwhile the rest of us scratch our heads and wonder how he can miss the obvious, every single time.) It's as though these people have to fall in every pothole in the street because it never occurs to them to go down a different road.

Are you smiling yet? Is someone in particular coming clearly into focus? Now, hold that thought.

God's Word says wisdom is truly a gift since it comes from the mouth of God, from the very words He speaks. And all God's Words have been written down for us, through the inspiration of the Holy Spirit. Therefore, those who refuse to accept God's guidance, who refuse to ask for His wisdom—those hapless relatives, perhaps—will never see the light of reality.

Know that if you hold fast to the precepts contained in the Bible, you will walk in integrity. Instead of gravitating toward potholes, your feet will be planted on the straight and narrow road.

From *Daily Wisdom for Women*
BY CAROL L. FITZPATRICK

FAITH IS. . .

Now FAITH is the assurance
(the confirmation, the title deed)
of the things [we] hope for,
being the proof of things [we] do not see
and the conviction of their reality.

Hebrews 11:1 Amplified

What do I need today? I can go ahead and list each item: faith, security, hope, wisdom, direction, peace, health, strength, friends, money, time. . .

Now, what do I need today that my heavenly Father cannot or will not provide? He promised all I need. There are no limitations on the word *all*. It stands alone in perfect completeness. All. And it is mine through faith.

This does not mean mindlessness, but rather freedom from worry about matters I cannot control. It is an assurance, quiet and contented, and is an evidence that God is. It is proof that His Word is living truth, effective in my heart and in my life because I believe.

What proof can I claim, when I do not yet have the actual item at hand? I claim God's Word, assert that if God says it is mine, it is. Faith is contentment with what I have now, and quiet expectancy of having what I may need in a moment or a day or a year. It is mine by title deed; my name is on the contract, and it will be available for my use at the exact moment I need it.

Faith is trusting my future, from now to the next moment and to forever, unto my heavenly Father's wisdom. Faith lived out is visible evidence of things not seen!

From *All I Have Needed*
by Elva Minette Martin

THE OCEANS OBEY THE LORD

The LORD reigneth, he is clothed with majesty;
the LORD is clothed with strength,
wherewith he hath girded himself:
the world also is stablished,
that it cannot be moved.

PSALM 93:1 KJV

Oh Lord, You are mightier than the huge breakers crashing against the ocean rocks. No other is greater than You! You display Your faithfulness in the cycle of the tides. How magnificent is the way their waves rise and fall at Your command. You shout and they rise. You whisper, they drift softly back into the ocean's depths. How do You cause the waters to stop at the shore? This water, soft as silk and harder than bricks, obeys Your will.

I walk along the sandy beach. I gaze out over the deep waters and recall the turbulence in my own life. Thank You for bringing my storms under control. Your mighty hand snatched me out of trials and tribulations; You have never dropped me.

As I stand gazing at Your marvelous creation, I dig my toes in the sand. The strong wind whips my hair. My tongue savors the salty air. I breathe deeply. Clean, cool air fills my lungs. Your refreshing Spirit surrounds me. You honor me with Your presence. I tremble at the thought of Your greatness.

Thank You for Your creation. Thank You, God, for life.

From *When I'm on My Knees*
BY ANITA CORRINE DONIHUE

I WANT TO LEAVE
MY MARK FOR THE LORD

I press on toward the goal to win the prize
for which God has called me
heavenward in Christ Jesus.

PHILIPPIANS 3:14 NIV

I know not what each day holds, or what time I have left to serve. This I do know, dear Lord, I want to leave my mark for You.

Help me make every day count. Remind me to lay aside my own wants, to be willingly inconvenienced and used for You. Let me not put anything before You, no matter how good it seems. Help me shed bad habits that slow me down from doing Your will.

I can only leave my mark for You by replacing idle time with purposeful movement. When I rest, I open my heart that You may fill me with Your strength and spirit.

Teach me to let go of yesterday, live fully today, and look with excitement toward tomorrow. I am awed as I daily come to know You more. I feel You shower love upon me like a refreshing summer rain.

Even though I am unworthy, I long to reach the end of life's journey and see You face-to-face. In the meantime, Lord, may I use each day, each hour, each moment to leave my mark for You. Amen.

From *When I'm on My Knees*
BY ANITA CORRINE DONIHUE

WHEN JESUS PRAYED FOR ME

"I have given them the glory that you gave me,
that they may be one as we are one:
I in them and you in me.
May they be brought to complete unity to let
the world know that you sent me
and have loved them even as you have loved me."

JOHN 17:22–23 NIV

*W*hen You were here on earth, Lord Jesus, You pleaded to Your Father for each one of us. I thank You and praise You for that. I can't imagine the agony You must have felt at that time, the tears You must have shed for our lost souls. I lift my heart in gratefulness because I'm allowed to know You as my Savior and Lord! I long to know You better. I am awed at how anxious You are to respond each time I come to You in prayer. You are more faithful than morning. In joy and trial I can come to You. You are here with me all the time.

Each time I align myself with Your will, I'm able to bring You my needs in faith, believing. In turn, I thank You for listening intently and taking them to Your heavenly Father on my behalf.

My prayers to You carry much power, but that power and magnitude come from You when You intercede for me to God. Thank You for all You do for me. Yours, dear Lord, are the kingdom and power and the glory forever.

From *When I'm Praising God*
BY ANITA CORRINE DONIHUE

THIS SPECIAL DAY

She watches over the affairs of her household
and does not eat the bread of idleness.
Her children arise and call her blessed;
her husband also, and he praises her.

PROVERBS 31:27–29 NIV

*L*ord, I collapse onto our couch, kick my shoes off, and think of today's blessings. Family and friends bustled around. Children chattered with youthful excitement. Steaming irresistible food simmered in the kitchen. Men exchanged stories and (thank You, Lord) helped with the little ones. It seems a whooshing dream; the day went so fast.

I reflect briefly on the struggles we've all had, the mountains we've fearfully conquered with Your help. Still we're together, loving and sharing. It was worth listening to each other and finding Your will through the years. I'm tired, but I loved it all. At nightfall, little arms wrapped around my neck with an "I love you, Nana." Strong embraces from sons so dear and tender hugs from loving daughters filled my heart with joy.

I thank You, Lord, for this day that You created and for the love of family and friends. As special days end in all their wild flurry, I'm often reminded of the true value in it all; not food, fancies, and elaborations, but my dearest friends and loved ones.

From *When I'm on My Knees*
BY ANITA CORRINE DONIHUE

If you enjoyed

JUST CALL ME MOM,

be sure to check out the following titles from
Barbour Publishing's Inspirational Library series:

All I Have Needed by Elva Minette Martin
The life of Elijah serves as an example and encouragement in this
forty-day devotional, providing essential insight in the nature of a
generous heavenly Father. 208 pages
ISBN 1-58660-136-9 . . . . $4.99

Created for a Purpose by Darlene Sala
This Bible-based encouragement book reminds women that God
loves each one of us and He has special plans for our lives. 224 pages
ISBN 1-57748-588-2 . . . . $4.99

Daily Wisdom for Women by Carol L. Fitzpatrick
Especially for women seeking biblical wisdom, this devotional chal-
lenges readers toward change with simple, relevant messages. 384 pages
ISBN 1-55748-937-8 . . . . $4.99

Encouraging Words for Women by Darlene Sala
In fifty-two devotional chapters, women are reminded of their worth
in God's eyes, of His protection, and of His guidance. 192 pages
ISBN 1-58660-492-9 . . . . $4.99

Everyday Abundance by Toni Sortor
These one hundred meditations, acknowledging God as the source
for "every good and perfect gift," draw upon Scripture to inspire a
greater sense of gratitude. 224 pages
ISBN 1-58660-570-4 . . . . $4.99

A Gentle Spirit compiled by Ashleigh Bryce Clayton
Emphasizing spiritual growth and personal development, this popular daily devotional draws upon the best writing of contemporary and classic Christian women. 384 pages
ISBN 1-57748-503-3 . . . . $4.99

Laughter Therapy by Tina Krause
More than four dozen hilarious essays offer humor "workouts" and spiritual lessons, designed to bring light to the less-than-amusing moments of a woman's life. 240 pages
ISBN 1-58660-513-5 . . . . $4.99

Lessons for a SuperMom by Helen Widger Middlebrooke
Lightheared, humorous, and occasionally poignant devotional essays for busy moms show that "washing dishes is just as holy as preaching sermons." 288 pages
ISBN 1-58660-495-3 . . . . $4.99

Stepping Heavenward by Elizabeth Prentiss
Hymn writer Elizabeth Prentiss penned this account of a girl who learns, on the path to womanhood, that true happiness is found in giving oneself for others. 352 pages
ISBN 1-57748-342-1 . . . . $4.99

Time Out by Leigh Ann Thomas
Especially for mothers of younger children, the encouraging devotional vignettes of *Time Out* are designed to say, "You're not alone." 208 pages
ISBN 1-57748-720-6 . . . . $4.99

You're Late Again, Lord! by Karon Phillips Goodman
Witty writing and thoughtful insights for any woman who's questioned God's timing, with encouragement to spend waiting time purposefully. 208 pages
ISBN 1-58660-410-4 . . . . $4.99

Available wherever books are sold.

BOOKS BY
ANITA CORRINE DONIHUE

When I'm on My Knees
Anita's first book, focusing on prayer, has sold more than a half-million copies.
    ISBN 1-55748-976-9 . . . . $4.99

When I'm Praising God
Anita's sequel to *When I'm on My Knees*, promoting praise as the key to a fulfilling Christian life.
    ISBN 1-57748-447-9 . . . . $4.99

When I'm in His Presence
Anita's third book, encouraging women to look for God's working in their everyday lives.
    ISBN 1-57748-665-X $4.99

When God Sees Me Through
Anita's fourth book in the series, celebrating the Lord's faithfulness through every circumstance of our lives.
    ISBN 1-57748-977-2 . . . . $4.99

When I Hear His Call
The fifth book in Anita's series offering challenge and encouragement to listen for, then respond to, God's call.
    ISBN 1-58660-279-9 . . . . $4.99

When God Calls Me Blessed
The sixth book in Anita's series focuses on the blessings of the Beatitudes.
    ISBN 1-58660-572-0 . . . . $4.99

Available wherever books are sold.
Or order from:

Barbour Publishing, Inc.
P.O. Box 719
Uhrichsville, OH 44683
www.barbourbooks.com

If you order by mail, add $2.00 to your order for shipping.
Prices are subject to change without notice.